KINGSTON UPON HU

BARTON-UPON-HUMBER · BEVERLEY

G000054328

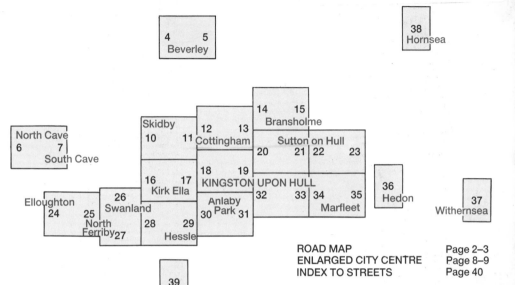

| 4   5 |
| Beverley |

38 Hornsea

14   15 Bransholme

Skidby
10   11

12   13 Cottingham

Sutton on Hull
20   21 22   23

North Cave
6   7
South Cave

16   17 Kirk Ella

18   19 KINGSTON UPON HULL
32   33 34   35

36 Hedon

37 Withernsea

Elloughton
24   25 Swanland
26
North Ferriby 27
28   29

Anlaby Park
30   31
Marfleet

Hessle

39 Barton-upon-Humber

ROAD MAP   Page 2–3
ENLARGED CITY CENTRE   Page 8–9
INDEX TO STREETS   Page 40

Every effort has been made to verify the accuracy of information in this book but the publishers cannot accept responsibility for expense or loss caused by an error or omission. Information that will be of assistance to the user of the maps will be welcomed.

The representation of a road, track or footpath on the maps in this atlas is no evidence of the existence of a right of way.

Car Park	℗
Public Convenience	©
Place of worship	✛
One-way Street	→
Pedestrianized	▨
Post Office	●

Scale of street plans 4 inches to 1 mile

Unless otherwise stated

Street plans prepared and published by ESTATE PUBLICATIONS, Bridewell House, TENTERDEN, KENT, and based upon the ORDNANCE SURVEY maps with the sanction of the Controller of H. M. Stationery Office.

The Publishers acknowledge the co-operation of Glanford B.C., The East Yorkshire Borough of Beverley, Holderness B.C. and Hull City Council.

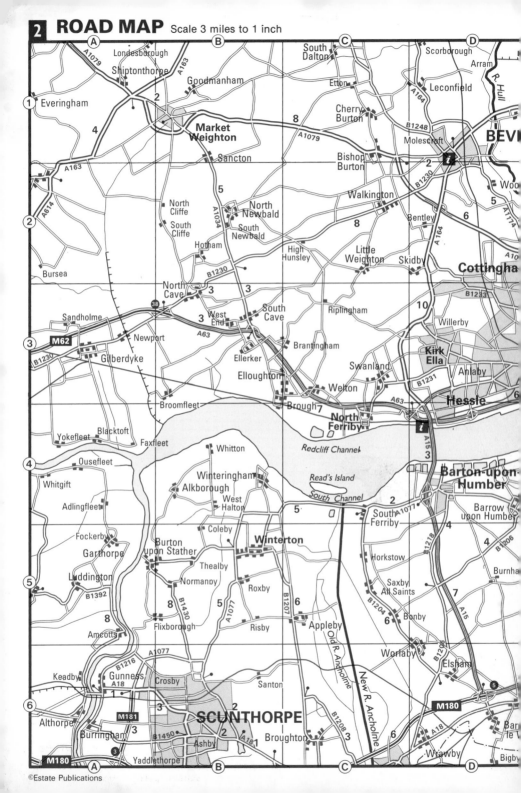

ROAD MAP Scale 3 miles to 1 inch

©Estate Publications

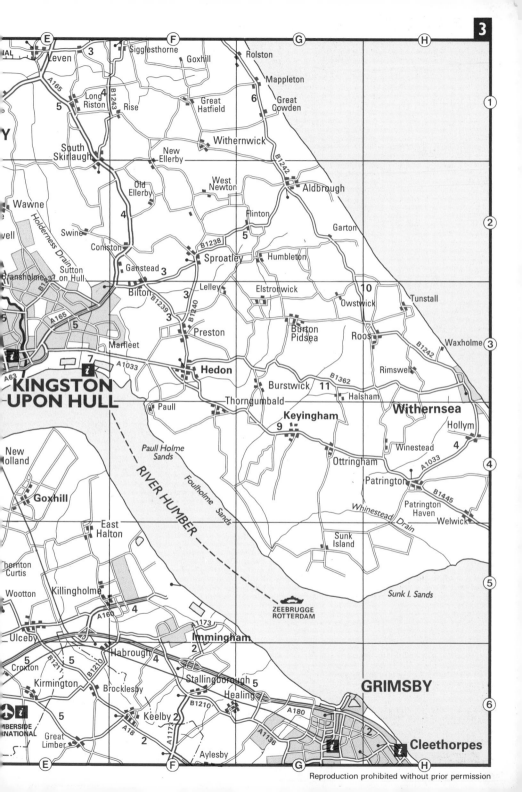

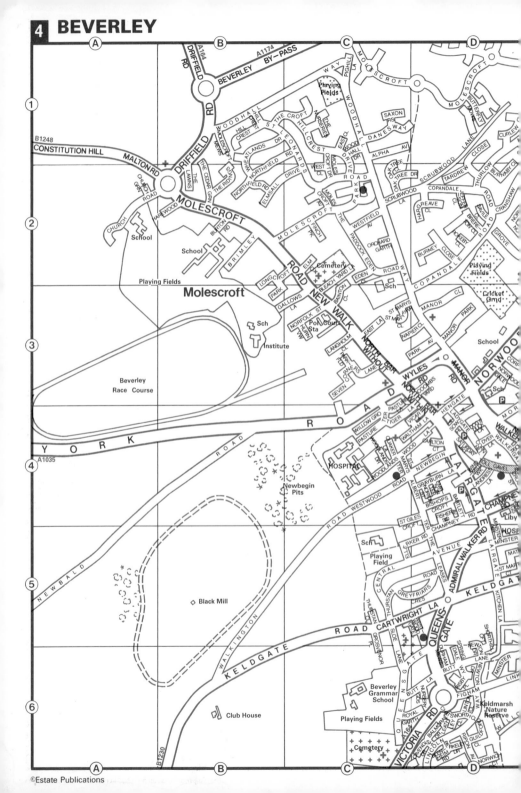

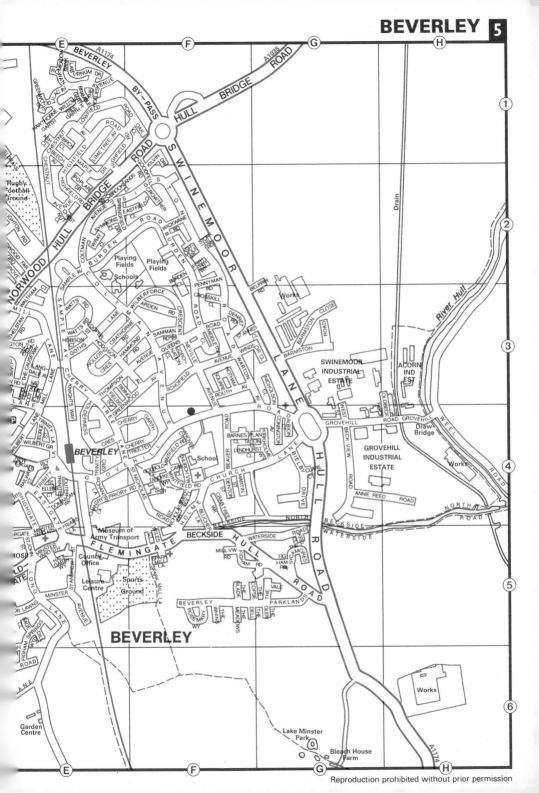

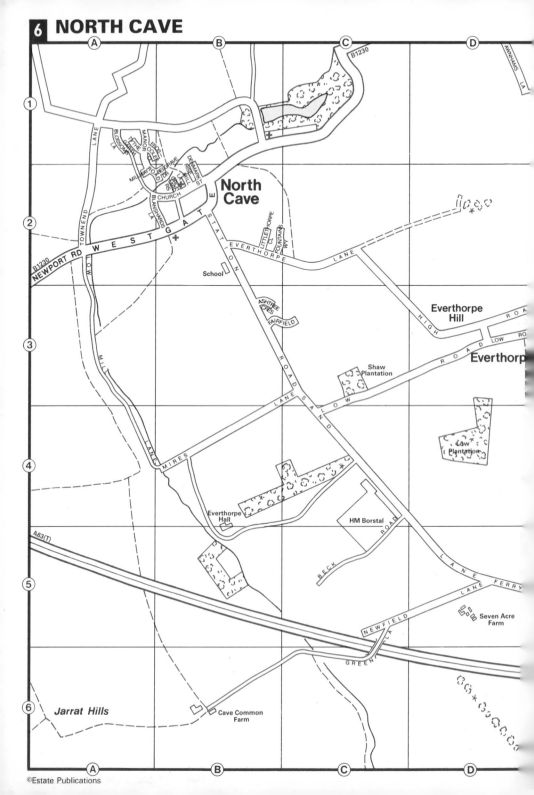

North Cave

Everthorpe
Hill

Everthorp

Everthorpe
Hall

HM Borstal

Shaw
Plantation

Low
Plantation

School

Seven Acre
Farm

Jarrat Hills

Cave Common
Farm

Newport Rd

WESTGATE

NEWPORT RD

B1230

A63(T)

B1230

©Estate Publications

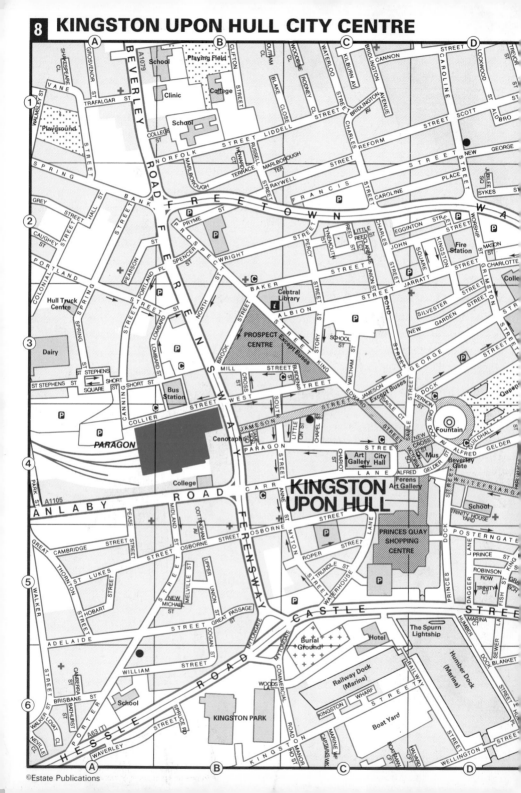

KINGSTON
UPON HULL

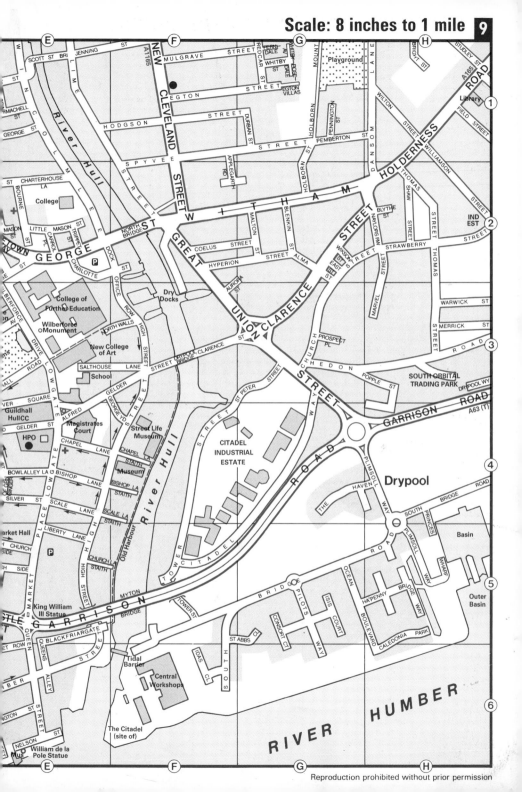

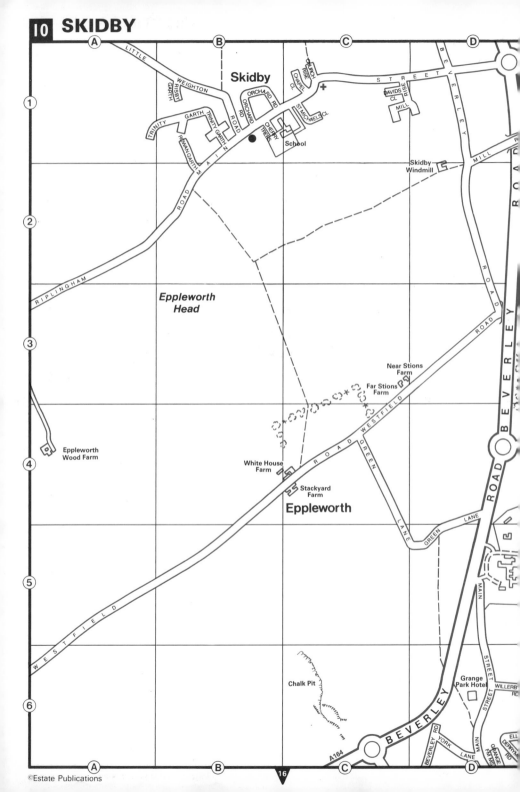

Skidby

LITTLE WEIGHTON
RISBY GARTH
TRINITY GARTH
TRINITY GARTH N
ROWANGARTH
MAIN ROAD
ORCHARD RD
ORCHARD RD
CHAPEL CL
CHURCH RISE
ST MICHAELS CL
CHERRY TREE RD
DAVIDS CL
MILL RISE
STREET
BEVERLEY
MILL ROAD

School

Skidby Windmill

RIPLINGHAM ROAD

Eppleworth Head

Near Stions Farm
Far Stions Farm

Eppleworth Wood Farm

WESTFIELD

White House Farm
Stackyard Farm

Eppleworth

WESTFIELD ROAD
GREEN LANE
GREEN LANE
BEVERLEY ROAD

Chalk Pit

Grange Park Hotel
MAIN STREET
WILLERB RD
BEVERLEY RD
YORK LANE
ELL DERINTM RD
GRANGE PK RD

BEVERLEY
A164

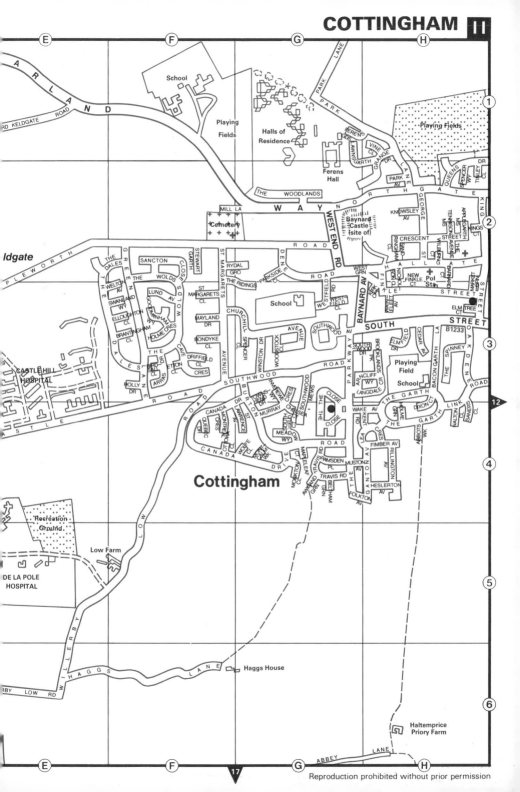

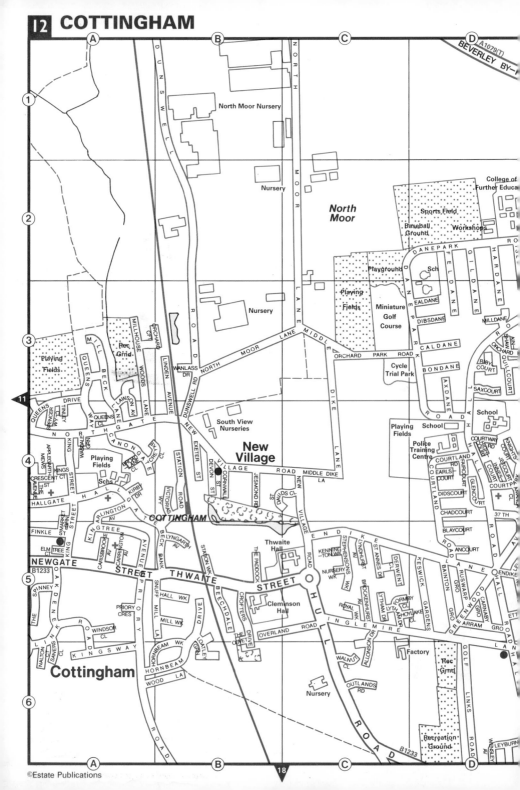

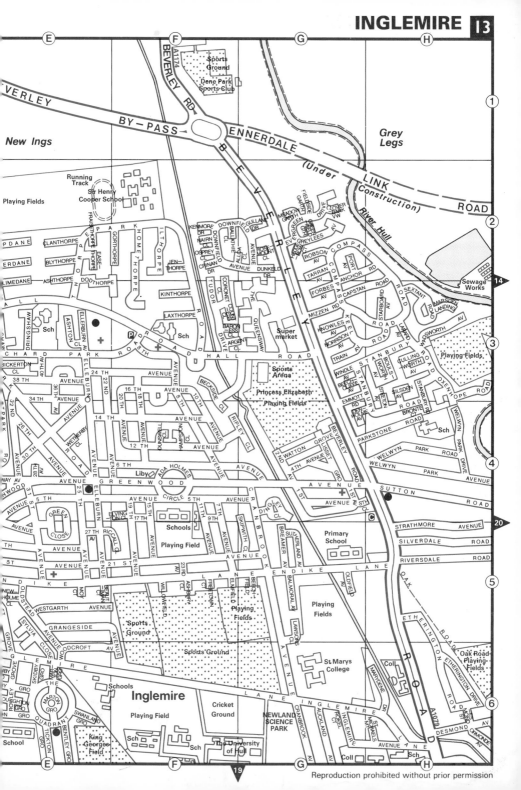

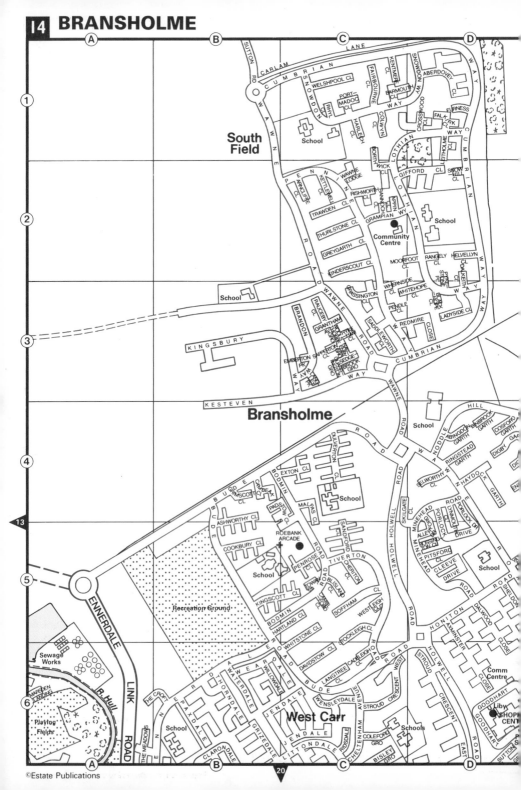

South Field

Bransholme

West Carr

Community Centre

School

Recreation Ground

Sewage Works

Playing Fields

Comm Centre

Roebank Arcade

Thirty Acre Farm

Hill Farm

High Bransholme

Low Bransholme

ROAD

Castle Hill

Playing Field

Bransholme Dairy Farm

BRANSHOLME

North Carr

Castle (site of)

ROAD

HUCKNALL GARTH

INNSWORTH GARTH

JASON GARTH

KINLOSS GARTH

LEEMING GARTH

MINSTON GARTH

School

Lambwath Hall

Playing Field

BIGGIN

AVENUE

BRENT GARTH

OAKINGDON GARTH

CASTLE HILL

Nursing Home

Schools

YEADON GARTH

WICKENBY GARTH

PATRINGTON GARTH

PINFORTH GARTH

SCAMPTON GARTH

TOPCLIFFE GARTH

UPAVON GARTH

KESTREL WAY

FULMAR

KINGFISHER CL

CROSS

ST

LAGOON

JAMES CL

ASTRAL

WAY

NODDLE HILL

Playground

CROFT

ST IVES

PERRAN CL

MADRON

ROAD

SUTTON

BOROUGH CL

MAPLE

CL

PEACK

CURLEW CL

LAPWING CL

KESTREL

MOBANK

DUNLIN

INNER DR

FOXHOLME

HOWDALE

ROAD

MERLIN CL

LAGOON

WHITSTABLE

TEAL

SITTINGBOURNE CL

RAMSGATE

BROAD

CANTERBURY

CLAYES

WHITSTABLE

DANBY

AVENUE

East Carr

Willerby Bottom

Kirk Ella

West Ella

Hull Golf Course

The Hall
(Club House)

St Andrews
Mount

School

Playing
Field

The Paddocks

Slights
Plantation

Four Acre
Plantation

Horseshoe
Plantation

Tranby
Courtyard

West Ella
Grange

Cemy

Cemy

Manor
Fields

A164

B1231 TRANBY

©Estate Publications

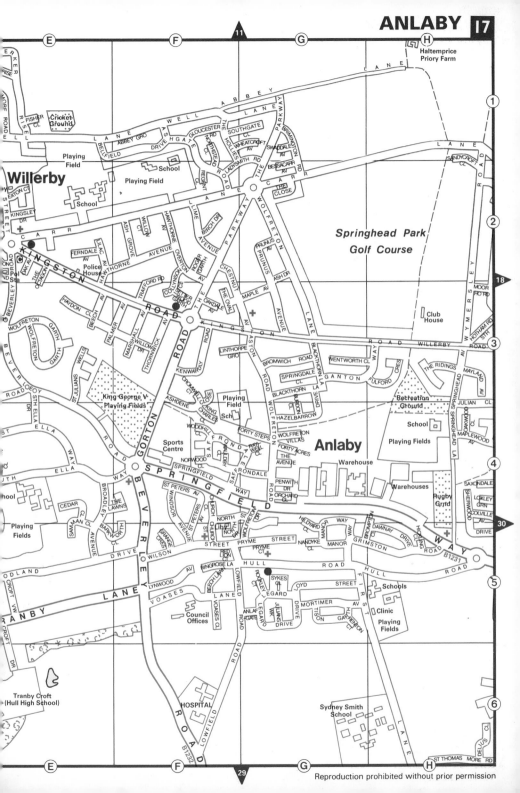

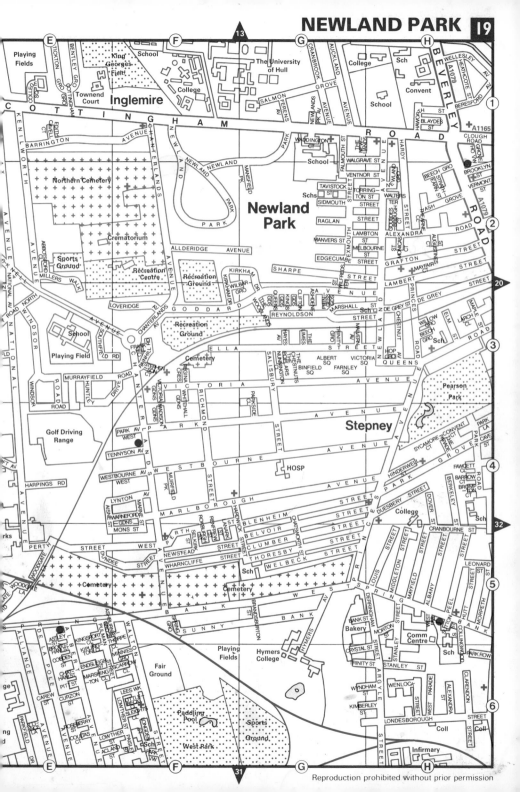

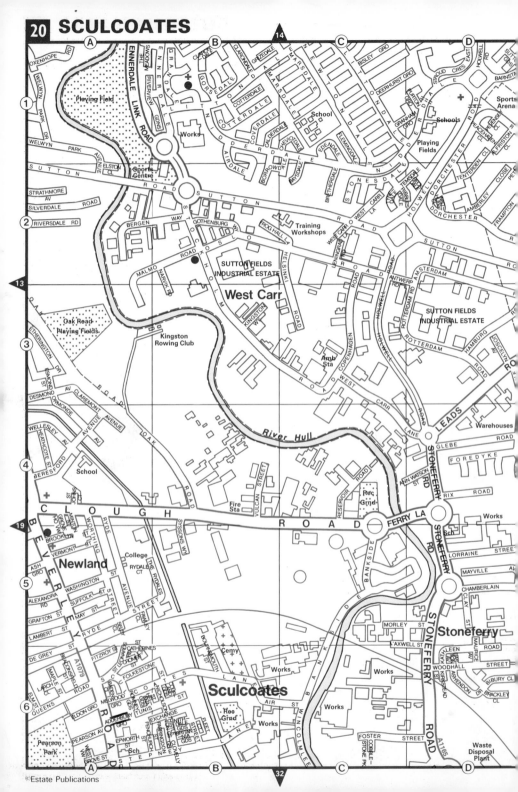

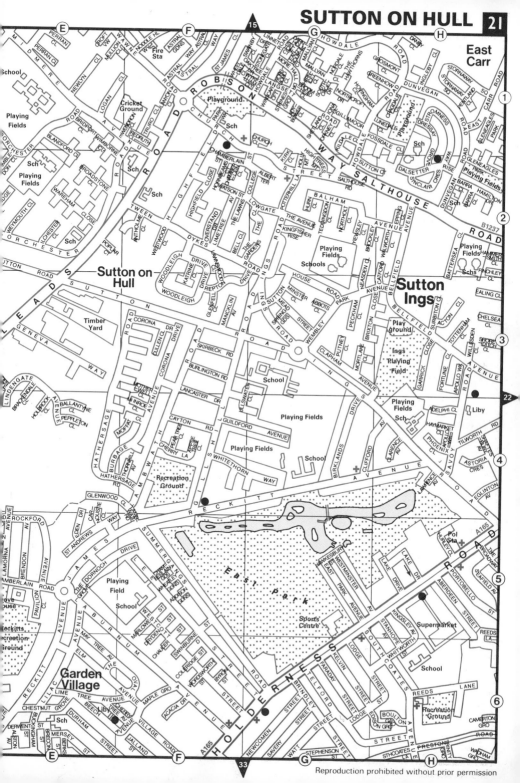

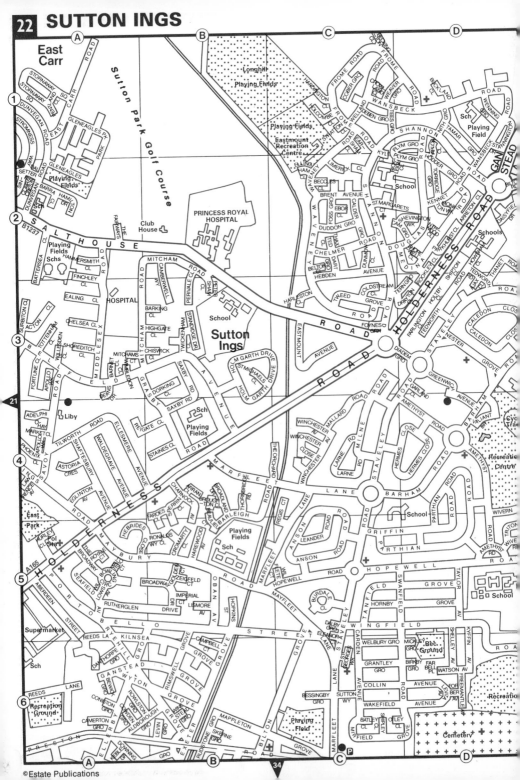

Bilton

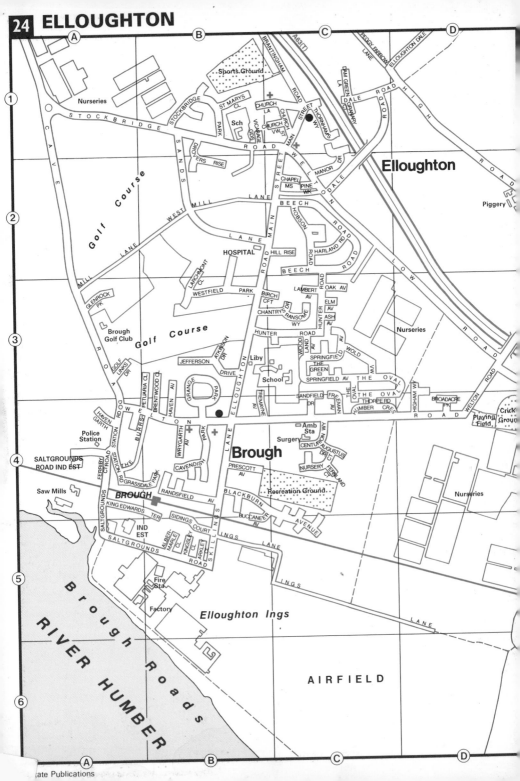

E · F · G · H

① Elloughton Wold

Welton Wold

Dale Plantation

Stonepit Plantation

Whiting Works

②

26

Bow Plantation

HIGH ROAD KIDD LANE
HALL WK
DALE WALK
STONEPIT ROAD
HILL LANE
BOW ROAD BOTTOM

Chapel CROSSALL HILL
HOLLY HILL
TEMPLE WK
TEMPLE CL
TEMPLE CL

③

COWGATE
INGMIRES GREEN
BECKSIDE CRES
ST GATE
LADYWELL
CHURCH
ST ANNES
WK
PARK RD
Welton
Sch

Melton Hill Farm
North Lawn

BARTRAMS
COWGTE SPRINGFIELD CL
ST HELENS DR
PARK RD
THE CRESCENT

Welton

WELTON OLD ROAD EAST DALE ROAD
MELTON ROAD

Sch

Playing Field

LOWFIELD LANE
School
POOLBANK LANE

ST JAMES DR
ST JAMES RD
REYNOLDS CL
GIBSON LA

Melton

South Lawn ④

27

LANE
COMMON
LANE

Nurseries

Pig Farm

A63(T)

MELTON FIELDS
BRICKYARD LANE

⑤

GREEN LANE

Low Field Farm

Works

Sports Ground

LOWFIELD LANE

Melton Common

COMMON LANE
LOW COMMON LANE

Humber Cement Works

GIBSON LANE

Smelting Works

⑥

E · F · G · H

Swanland

West Field Farm

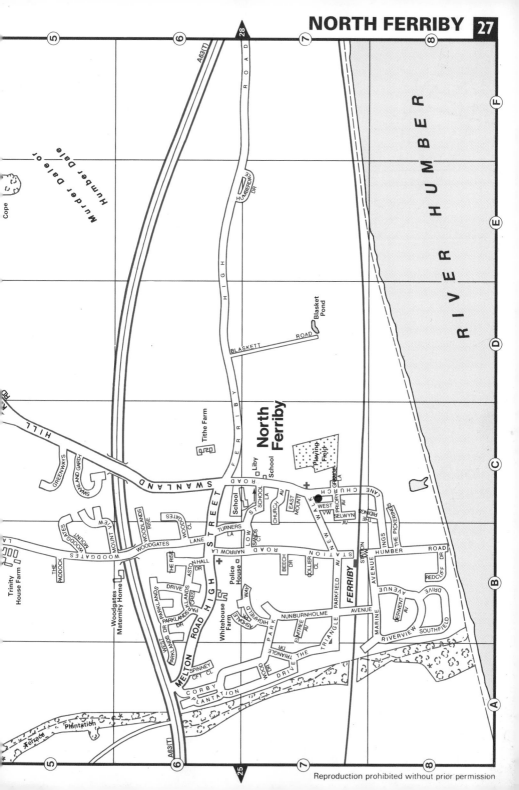

North Ferriby

RIVER HUMBER

Blasket Pond

Playing Field

Trinity House Farm

Tithe Farm

Cope

Murder Dale or Humber Dale

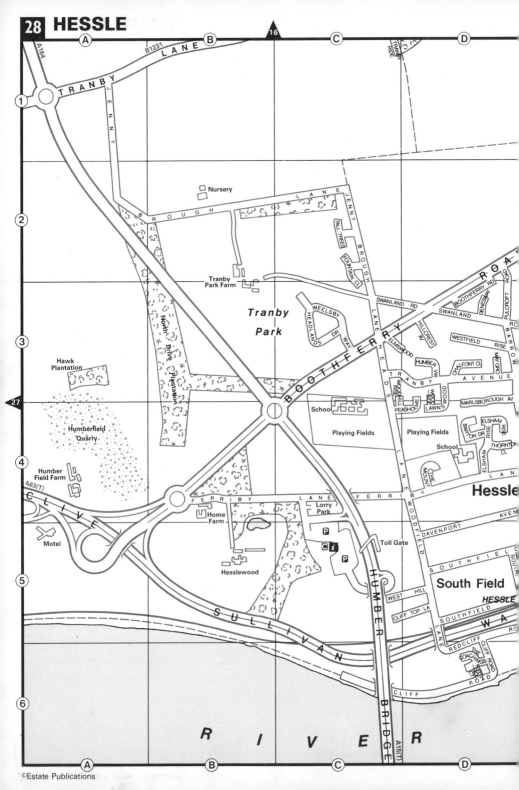

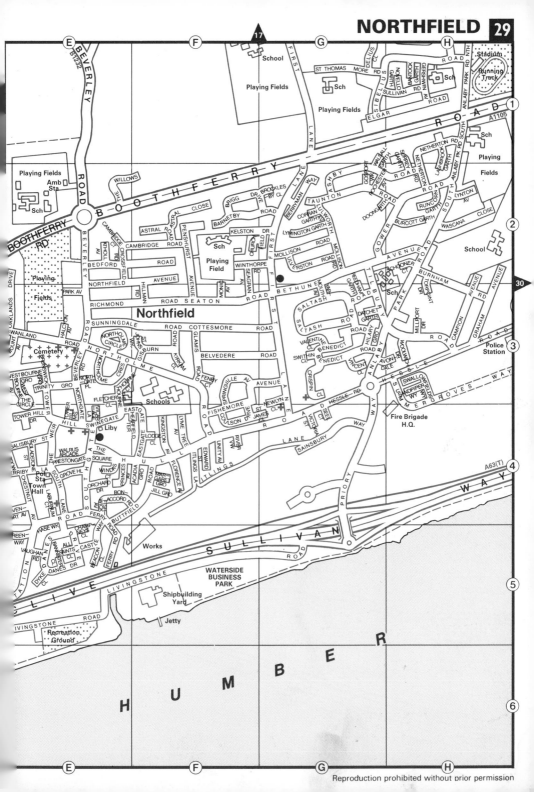

Northfield

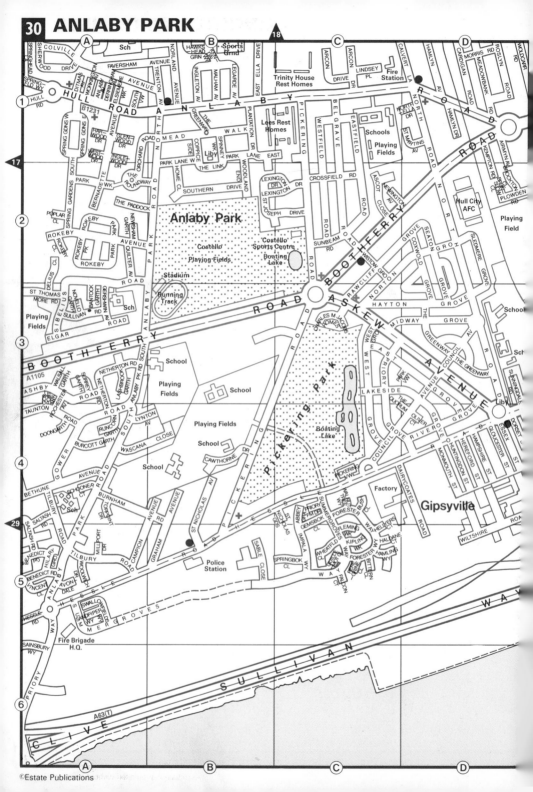

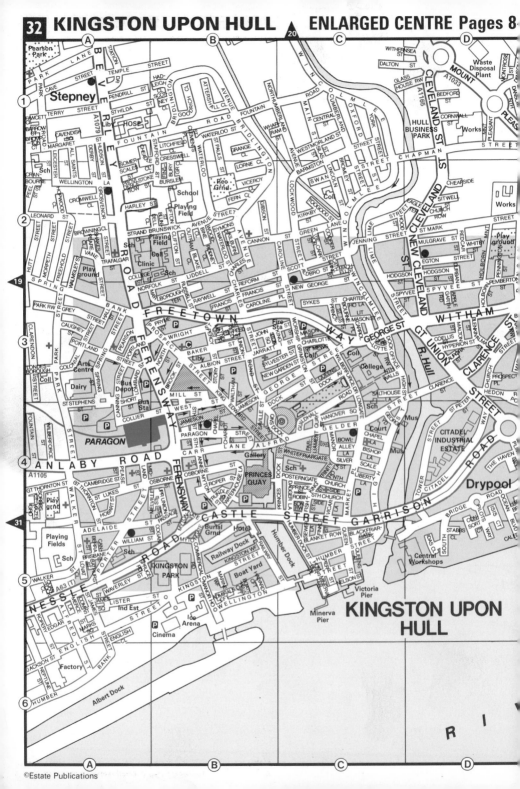

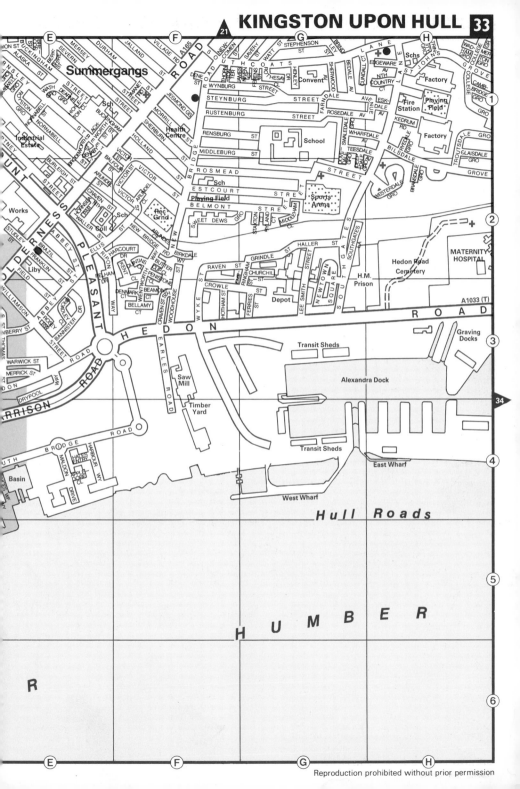

22

Marfleet

Schs
ST JOHNS
Factory
Playing Field
Factory
BILSDALE
BRANSDALE GRO
GROVE
COLLEGE
CAMBRIDGE
COLLEGE
PEMBROKE
GROVE
TROUTSDALE
GLAISDALE GRO
GROVE
GROVE
MERTIN GRO
DOWNING
CLARE GRO
ORIEL GRO
EXETER ST
FLINTON
ST JOHNS
WANSFORD
FOSTON
HARPHAM
HILTON
CRANSWICK
ATWICK
MOWBERRY
INGLAND CT
GROVE
BEWHOLME
GROVE
PRESTON
Liby
GRO
BRIGHAM
GROVE
GROVE
GROVE
HOLMPTON
School
Playing Fields
School
LANE
ROAD
Cemetery
ANNANDALE
School
POORHOUSE LA
Craven Park
(Rugby &
Greyhound Stadium)
POORHOUSE
GREAT FIELD LA

School
Playing Fields

Depot
MATERNITY HOSPITAL
Hedon Road Cemetery
Works
Works
Depot
LITTLEFAIR
ROAD
Wks
BURMA
DRIVE
MARFLEET AVENUE
MARFLEET LN
MARFLEET
DELHI ST
FRODSHAM ST
CYPRUS
EGYPT
CYPRUS WK
CYPRUS ST
Works
CEYLON
STREET
Recreation Ground
Schl
CHURCH
LANE
Works
Burial Ground
Works
Fact

HEDON ROAD
A1033(T)
Depot
CORPORATION RD
Graving Docks
Alexandra Dock
Transit Shed
Transit Shed
Transit Sheds
Transit Sheds
Ferry Terminal
Transit Shed
King George Dock
Transit Sh

33

Transit Shed
CORPORATION ROAD
P
Freight Terminal
Pier
Jetty
Fire Station
Pier
Locks
Transit Sheds
Queen Elizab Dock

R I V E R   H U M B E R

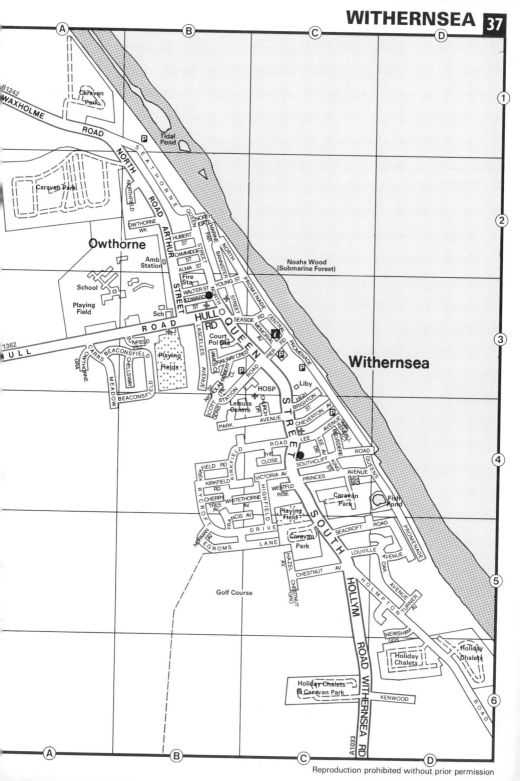

A B C D

1
2
3
4
5
6

B1242

WAXHOLME ROAD

Caravan Park

Caravan Park

NORTH ROAD

SEATHORNE

Tidal Pond

ARTHUR STREET

Owthorne

NORTHFIELD

OWTHORNE WK

School

Playing Field

Amb Station

Fire Sta

HUBERT ST

CAMMIDGE ST

ALMA ST

WALTER ST

EDWARD

Sch

QUEEN STREET

NORTH GATE

ALMARINE PSR

BANNISTER ST

YOUNG ST

NORTH STREET

HULL RD

ROAD

ULL

1362

CARRS

OWTHORNE GRA

BEACONSFIELD

CHELLSWAY

MEADOW

BEACONSFIELD

NORTHFIELD VILL

QUEEN STREET

LASCELLES AVENUE

Playing Fields

Court
Pol Sta

Leisure Centre

HOSP

SCOTT SONS CT

NICOLSON AV

ST ROBERT RD

JAMES CT

PARK

CHURCH AVENUE

SEASIDE RD

CENTRAL

MEMORIAL AV

PROMENADE

RAILWAY CRES

PIER

PROMENADE RD

Noahs Wood
(Submarine Forest)

Withernsea

Seaside

Liby

High

Brighton ST

CHEVERTON AV

LEE

AVENUE

BELVEDERE

KENDAL

LEE AV

KING AV

QUEENS AVENUE

ROAD

SOUTHCLIFF

SOUTH STREET

THE CLOSE

FIELD RD

PARK RD

KIRKFIELD RD

KIRKFIELD

CHERRY TREE AV

RYCROFT

WHITETHORNE AV

HIGHFIELD ROAD

VICTORIA AV

WESTFLD RISE

FRANCIS AV

PRINCES

Caravan Park

Fish Pond

NORMAN

EGROMS

DRIVE

LANE

Caravan Park

Playing Field

SEACROFT ROAD

HAZEL AV

CHESTNUT GRO

CHESTNUT AV

LOUVILLE AVENUE

OAK

Golf Course

HOLMPTON ROAD

HOLLYM ROAD

WITHERNSEA RD

A1033

PROMENADE

TURNER AV

NEWSHAM GDS

Holiday Chalets

Holiday Chalets

Holiday Chalets & Caravan Park

KENWOOD

ROAD

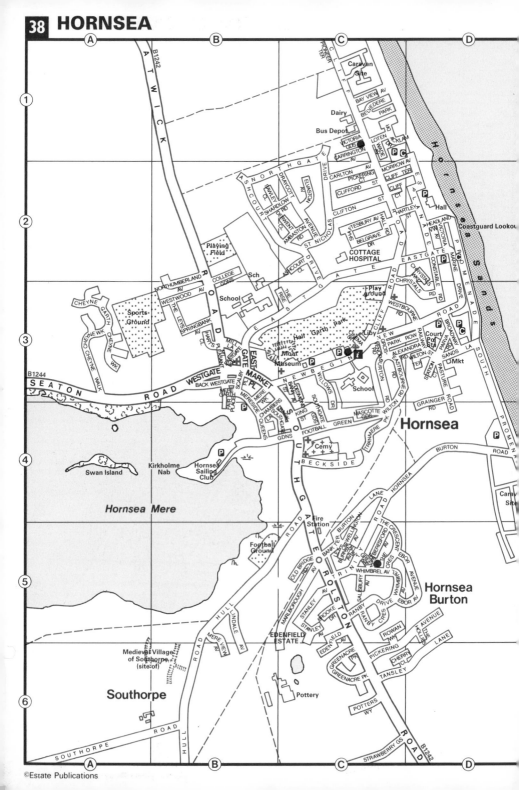

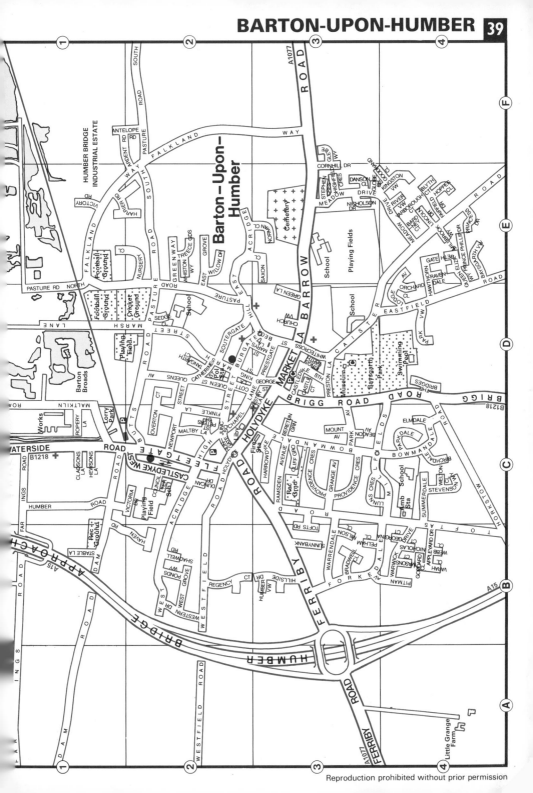

A - Z INDEX TO STREETS
with Postcodes

The Index includes some names for which there is insufficient space on the maps. These names are preceded by an * and are followed by the nearest adjoining thoroughfare.

KINGSTON UPON HULL

Bow Rd. HU14 25 G2
Bowes Wk. HU5 18 D2
Bowlalley La. HU1 9 E4
Bowling Circ HU9 22 A5
Boynton St. HU3 31 G3
Brackendale Clo. HU7 21 E3
Brackley Clo. HU8 20 D6
Bradford Av. HU9 23 E6
Braids Wk. HU10 16 C2
Brandon Wy. HU7 14 C3
Brandsby Gro. HU9 23 E5
Bransburton St. HU3 19 G5
Bransdale Gro. HU8 33 H2
Bransholme Rd. HU7 15 E4
Brantingham Clo.HU16 11 F3
Brantingham Rd. HU15 24 C1
Brantingham Wk. HU5 18 B3
Brazil St. HU9 33 E2
Breamer Av. HU6 13 G5
*Brecon Av,
  Brecon St. HU8 21 E6
Brecon St. HU8 21 E6
Brendon Av. HU8 21 E5
*Brentwood Av,
  Brazil St. HU9 33 E2
*Brentwood Av,
  Hardwick St. HU5 19 F4
Brentwood Clo.HU15 24 B4
*Brentwood Villas,
  Perry St. HU3 31 F1
*Brentwood Villas,
  Reynoldson St. HU5 19 G3
Bretherdale. HU7 20 C2
Briarfield Rd. HU5 19 E3
Bricknell Av. HU5 19 E2
Brickyard La. HU14 25 H5
Bridlington Av. HU12 8 C1
Bridport Rd. HU7 21 E1
Brigg Dri. HU13 29 F2
Brigham Gro. HU9 34 B1
Bright St. HU8 33 E2
Brighton St. HU4 31 E4
Brimington Rd. HU10 17 G1
Brindley St. HU9 21 G6
Brisbane St. HU3 8 A6
Bristol Rd. HU5 18 B4
Britannia Rds. HU5 20 B6
*Brixham Ct,
  Edinburgh St. HU3 31 F2
Brixton Clo. HU8 21 G3
Broad Oak. HU11 23 E2
Broadacre Pk. HU15 24 D4
Broadland Dri. HU6 22 B4
Broadlane Clo.HU16 12 A4
Broadley Av. HU10 17 E4
Broadley Clo. HU9 33 E3
Broadstairs Clo. HU16 15 G6
Broadstone Clo. HU7 21 E2
Broadway Dri. HU8 22 B5
Brockenhurst Av. HU16 12 C5
Brocklesby Clo. HU13 29 G2
Brockley Clo. HU8 21 G2
Brockton Clo. HU3 30 D2
Brodsworth St. HU8 33 E1
Bromley St. HU2 32 C2
Brompton Clo,
  Anlaby. HU10 17 G5
Brompton Clo,
  Hull. HU5 19 H4
Brompton Ct. HU3 19 H4
Bromwich Rd. HU10 17 G3
Bronte Ct. HU6 13 H4
Brook St. HU1 8 B3
Brooklands Pk. HU16 11 H3
Brooklands Rd. HU5 18 D5
*Brooklyn Av,
  Brooklyn St. HU5 20 A5
*Brooklyn Av,
  Perth St. HU5 19 F5
Brooklyn St. HU5 20 A5
*Brooklyn Ter,
  Worthing St. HU5 20 A5
*Brooklyn Villas,
  Ceylon St. HU9 34 C3
Broomhead Clo. HU8 21 G1
Brougham St. HU3 19 F6
Broughton Clo. HU3 32 A2
Browning Clo. HU3 32 A2
Brucella Gro. HU9 31 F3
*Brumbys Ter,
  Craven St Sth. HU9 33 F4
Brunslow Clo. HU3 30 D2
*Brunswick Av,
  Waterloo St. HU2 32 B2
*Brunswick Av,
  St Georges St. HU3 31 F2
Brunswick Av,
  Franklin St. HU9 33 E2
*Brunswick Clo. HU13 29 E3
Buccaneer Av. HU15 24 B5
Buckingham St. HU8 21 E6
Buckland Clo. HU8 22 D1
Bude Rd. HU7 14 B4
Burbage Av. HU8 21 E4
Burcott Garth. HU4 29 H2

Burdale Clo. HU9 22 C5
Burden St. HU1 8 C3
Burdon Clo. HU10 17 G4
Burleigh St. HU8 33 E2
Burlington Rd. HU3 21 F3
Burma Dri. HU9 34 B2
Burnby Clo. HU5 18 B3
Burnham Rd. HU4 29 H2
Burniston Rd. HU5 18 D3
Burrill Mws. HU5 18 D1
Burslem St. HU2 32 B2
Burton Rd. HU4 11 G3
Bush Clo. HU4 30 C4
Buttercup Clo. HU9 33 F2
Buttfield Rd. HU13 29 E4
*Buxton Villas,
  Rosmead St. HU9 33 F2
Byland Ct. HU4 33 G2
Byron St. HU8 21 F6
Cadeleigh Clo. HU7 14 C6
*Cadogan Av,
  Cadogan St. HU3 31 G2
*Cadogan Gro,
  Cadogan St. HU3 31 G2
Caldane. HU6 12 D3
Caldberg Mws. HU5 18 C2
Calder Gro. HU8 22 C2
Calderdale. HU7 20 B1
Caledon Gro. HU3 22 D3
Caledonia Pk. HU9 9 H5
Calthorpe Gdns,
  Newington St. HU3 31 E2
Calthorpe St. HU3 31 G2
Calvert La. HU4 18 B6
Calvert Rd. HU5 18 C4
Cam Gro. HU8 22 D2
Cambeak Clo. HU7 14 B4
Camberwell Way. HU8 22 B2
Camborne Gro. HU8 20 D5
*Cambrian Av,
  Holland St. HU9 33 F1
Cambridge Ct. HU13 29 E2
Cambridge Gro. HU3 34 A1
Cambridge Rd. HU13 29 E2
Cambridge St. HU3 8 A5
Camden St. HU3 31 G2
Camelford Clo. HU7 14 C5
Camerton Gro. HU7 22 A6
Campbell St. HU9 22 B6
Campbell St. HU3 31 H2
Camper Down. HU11 23 E2
Campion Av. HU4 29 H3
Canada Dri. HU16 11 F4
Canberra St. HU3 8 A6
Canning St. HU1 8 A4
Cannon St. HU2 8 C1
Canongate. HU16 12 A4
Canopias St. HU3 31 F3
Canterbury Dri. HU8 15 G6
Capstan Rd. HU4 13 G3
Captains Wk. HU1 8 C6
Carden Av. HU3 22 C6
*Cardigan Av,
  De la Pole Av. HU3 19 E5
*Cardigan Av,
  Fenchurch St. HU5 20 A6
Cardigan Rd. HU3 30 D1
Carew St. HU3 19 E6
Carisbrooke Av. HU16 12 A5
*Carisbrooke Av,
  De la Pole Av. HU3 19 E5
*Carisbrook Av,
  Manvers St.HU5 19 G2
*Carisbrook Villas,
  Montrose St. HU8 32 D1
*Carisbrook Villas,
  Reynoldson St. HU5 19 G3
*Carlton Av,
  Reynoldson St. HU5 19 G3
Carlam La. HU7 14 B1
*Carlisle Av,
  Albemarle St. HU3 31 F2
*Carlton Av,
  Frodsham St. HU9 34 B2
Carlton St. HU3 31 E3
*Carlton Villas,
  Goddard Av. HU5 19 G3
*Carlton Villas,
  Greek St. HU3 31 F3
Carnaby Gro. HU6 12 D5
*Carnegie St,
  Perry St. HU3 31 F1
Carnoustie Clo. HU8 21 E5
Carol Dickson Ct. HU3 31 H2
Caroline Pl. HU2 8 C2
Caroline St. HU2 8 D1
Carperby Mws. HU5 18 C1
Carr La. Hull. HU1 8 B4
Carr La. Willerby. HU10 17 E2
Carr St. HU2 8 D1
Carrington Av. HU16 12 A5
*Carrington Av,
  De la Pole Av. HU3 19 E5
*Carrington Av,
  Manvers St. HU5 19 G2

Carrington St. HU3 31 G2
Carrol Pl. HU2 9 E2
*Castle Gro,
  Perth St West. HU5 19 F5
Castle Rd HU16 11 E4
Castle St. HU1 8 C5
Castle Way. HU13 29 E5
Castleford Gro. HU3 35 F1
Castlehill Rd. HU7 15 F5
Castleton Av. HU5 18 C2
Catford Clo. HU8 21 H3
*Catherine Gro,
  Carrington St. HU3 31 G2
Catherine St. HU2 9 E1
Caughey St. HU2 8 A2
Cave Cres. HU16 24 A1
Cave Rd. HU15 24 A1
Cave St. HU5 32 A1
Cavendish Pk. HU15 24 B4
Cavendish Sq. HU3 32 A1
Cavill Pl. HU3 31 H2
*Cawood Av,
  Filed St. HU9 9 H1
Cawthorne Dri. HU4 30 B4
Cayton Rd. HU8 21 F4
Cecil St. HU3 31 E2
Cedar Av. HU16 11 H3
Cedar Clo. HU10 17 E4
*Cedar Gro,
  Estcourt St. HU9 33 F2
*Cedar Gro,
  New St. HU3 31 E2
Cedarwood Dri. HU5 18 A6
Celandine Clo. HU5 18 C4
Central St. HU2 32 C1
Centurion Way. HU15 24 C4
Ceylon St. HU9 34 C2
Chadcourt. HU6 12 D4
Chalfont Clo. HU13 28 D3
Chamberlain Av. HU7 21 F2
Chamberlain Gdns. HU8 21 F5
Chamberlain Rd. HU8 20 D5
Champneys Clo. HU13 29 E5
Chanterlands Av. HU5 19 F1
Chantry Av. HU14 26 D3
Chantry Way
  East. HU14 26 D3
Chantrys Dri. HU15 24 B3
Chapel Clo. HU16 10 C1
Chapel Hill. HU15 25 E3
Chapel La, Hull. HU1 9 E4
Chapel La,
  West Ella. HU10 16 B4
Chapel La Staith. HU1 9 F4
Chapel Ms. HU15 24 C2
Chapel St. HU1 8 C4
Chapman St. HU1 32 D1
Chariot St. HU1 8 C4
Charles M. Jacobs
  Homes. HU4 30 C3
Charles St. HU2 8 C1
Charlotte St. HU1 9 E2
Charlotte St Mws. HU1 8 D2
*Charton Villas,
  Estcourt St. HU9 33 F2
Charnock Av. HU4 22 B4
Charter Field. HU11 23 E2
Charterhouse La. HU2 9 E2
*Chatham Av,
  Manvers St. HU5 19 G2
Chatham St. HU3 19 E6
*Chatsworth Av,
  Welbeck St. HU5 19 G5
*Chatsworth Av,
  Manvers St. HU5 19 G2
Chaucer St .HU8 21 F6
Cheadle Clo. HU2 32 A1
Cheapside. HU8 32 D2
Chelmer Rd. HU8 22 C2
Chelmsford Clo. HU9 35 F1
Chelsea Clo. HU8 22 A3
Chelsea Ct. HU16 11 G4
Cheltenham Av. HU7 14 C6
Cheriton Clo. HU4 14 C5
Cherry Garth. HU3 31 F2
Cherry La. HU8 21 F4
Cherry Tree Av. HU8 21 F6
Cherry Trees. HU16 10 B1
Cheshire Clo. HU5 18 C4
*Chester Av,
  Fenchurch St. HU5 20 A6
*Chester Av,
  Manvers St. HU5 19 G2
*Chester Gro,
  Albemarle St. HU3 31 F2
Chester Holme. HU1 23 E2
Chester Rd. HU5 18 A3
Chestnut Av.
  Willerby. HU10 17 F2
*Chestnut Av,
  Montrose St. HU8 32 D1
*Chestnut Av,
  New St. HU3 31 E2

Chestnut Gro. HU8 21 E6
Cheviotdale. HU7 20 C1
Chevy Chase. HU7 23 E2
Chiltern St. HU3 31 G2
Chilton Rise. HU10 16 D2
Chiswick Clo. HU4 22 B3
Cholmley St. HU3 31 G2
Church Av. HU14 27 C7
Church Clo,
  Anlaby. HU10 17 F4
Church Clo,
  Sutton-on-Hull. HU7 21 G1
Church Field. HU13 29 F2
Church La, Bilton. HU11 23 F2
Church La,
  Elloughton. HU15 24 C1
Church La,
  Kirk Ella. HU10 16 D3
Church La,
  Marfleet. HU9 34 C2
Church La Staith. HU1 9 E5
Church Rise. HU16 10 C1
Church Road. HU14 27 C7
Church Row. HU8 32 D2
Church St,
  Anlaby. HU10 17 F5
Church St,
  Elloughton. HU15 24 C1
Church St, Hull. HU9 9 G3
Church St,
  Sutton-on-Hull. HU7 21 F1
Church St,
  Welton. HU15 25 E3
Church Vw HU15 24 C1
Churchill Av. HU16 11 F3
*Churchill Av, De la
  Pole Av. HU3 19 E5
*Churchill Gro,
  Alexandra Rd. HU5 19 H2
Churchill St. HU9 33 G2
*Churchill Villas,
  Holland St. HU9 33 F1
Citadel Way. HU9 9 F5
Cladshaw. HU6 13 E3
Clairbrook Clo. HU3 31 F2
Clanthorpe. HU6 13 E2
Clapham St. HU3 21 G3
Clare Gro. HU9 34 B1
Claremont Av. HU6 20 A3
*Claremont Av,
  Reynoldson St. HU5 19 G3
*Claremont Av,
  Selkirk St. HU5 19 F5
*Clarence Av,
  Delhi St. HU9 34 B2
Clarence Ct. HU2 8 C3
Clarence St. HU9 9 G3
*Clarendon Av,
  Manvers St. HU5 19 G2
Clarendon St. HU3 19 H6
Clarondale. HU7 20 B1
Clay St. HU8 20 D5
Cleeve Dri. HU7 14 D5
Cleveland St. HU8 32 D1
Cliff Rd. HU13 28 D6
Cliff Top La. HU13 28 D5
Clifford Av. HU8 21 G4
*Clifton Gdns,
  St Georges Rd. HU3 31 F2
Clifton Gdns. HU5 19 G3
Clifton St. HU2 32 B2
*Clinton Av,
  Manvers St. HU5 19 G2
Clive Sullivan
  Way. HU13 29 E5
*Clive Vale,
  Estcourt St. HU9 33 F2
*Clivedale Av,
  Edgecumbe St. HU5 19 G2
Clough Rd. HU6 20 A4
Cloughton Gro. HU5 18 D3
*Clovelly Av,
  De la Pole Av. HU3 19 E5
*Clovelly Av,
  Edgecumbe St. HU5 19 G2
Clovelly Gdns. HU5 20 B6
Cloverbank Vw. HU6 13 G2
Clumber St. HU5 19 G5
Clyde St. HU3 31 E2
*Clydesdale Av,
  Clyde St. HU3 31 E2
Cobblestone Pk. HU5 20 C6
Cobden St. HU3 19 E6
Cober Gro. HU8 22 C1
Cock Pit Clo. HU10 16 D5
Coelus St. HU9 9 F2
Cogan St. HU1 8 B5
Coldstream Clo. HU8 22 C3
Coleford Gro. HU7 14 C6
*Colenso Av,
  Holland St. HU9 33 F1
Colenso St. HU9 33 F1
*Colenso Villas,
  Barnsley St. HU8 33 E1

Coleridge St. HU8 21 F6
College Gro. HU9 34 A1
College Sq. HU6 19 E1
College St, Hull. HU2 8 A1
College St,
  Sutton-on-Hull. HU7 21 F2
Collier Clo. HU14 27 B7
Collier St. HU1 8 A4
Collin Av. HU9 22 C6
Collingwood St. HU3 19 H5
Collynson Clo. HU10 17 F2
Colonial St. HU2 8 A3
Coltman St. HU3 31 G1
Colville Av. HU4 18 A6
Colwall Av. HU5 18 C2
Colwyn Clo. HU4 14 C1
Commerce La. HU1 32 A5
Commercial Rd.HU1 8 C6
Common La. HU15 25 E5
Compass Rd. HU6 13 G2
Conifer Clo. HU5 18 B5
Coniston Gro. HU9 22 A6
Constable Av. HU11 23 G1
Constable St. HU3 31 G2
Convent Ct. HU5 19 H4
Convent La. HU3 31 H1
Conway Clo. HU3 31 G2
Cookbury Clo. HU7 14 B5
Cooper St. HU2 32 C2
Copenhagen Rd. HU7 20 C3
Copper Beech
  Clo. HU4 26 A4
Coppice Side. HU4 30 B1
Corbridge Clo. HU3 35 E1
Corby Pk. HU14 27 A6
Cordella Clo. HU3 31 F2
Cormorant Clo. HU7 15 F6
*Cornwall Gdns,
  Raglan St. HU5 19 G2
*Cornwall Gdns,
  Wellsted St. HU3 31 G2
Cornwall St,
  Cottingham. HU16 12 B4
Cornwall St. Hull. HU8 32 D1
Corona Dri. HU8 21 F3
*Coronation Av,
  Rustenburg St. HU9 33 F1
Coronation Rd Nth. HU5 18 B3
Coronation Rd Sth. HU5 18 A4
Coronet Gro. HU6 13 F3
Corporation Rd. HU9 32 C5
Corran Garth. HU4 29 G2
Corsair Gro. HU3 31 F3
Cosford Garth. HU7 14 D4
Cottage Dri. HU10 16 C4
Cotterdale. HU7 20 B1
Cottesmore Rd. HU13 29 F3
Cottingham Av. HU1 8 B5
Cottingham Gro. HU6 19 E1
Cottingham Rd. HU6 18 D1
Coulson Dri. HU13 29 F4
Coultas St. HU3 19 E6
Council Av. HU4 30 C4
Countess Clo. HU6 13 F3
County Rd Nth. HU5 18 C4
County Rd Sth. HU5 18 B5
Coupland Gdns. HU5 20 B6
Courtland Rd. HU6 12 D4
Courtney St. HU8 33 E1
Courtpark Rd. HU6 12 D4
Courtway Rd. HU6 12 D4
Coventry Rd. HU5 18 B4
Coverdale. HU7 20 B1
Cowden Gro. HU9 22 A6
Cowgate. HU15 25 E3
Coxwold Gro. HU4 30 D2
Cradley Rd. HU4 18 C2
Cragdale Clo. HU8 21 H1
*Cranbourne Av,
  Fenchurch St. HU5 20 A6
Cranbourne St. HU3 19 H5
Cranbrook Av. HU6 13 G4
Cranswick Gro. HU9 34 B1
Craven St Nth. HU9 33 F3
Craven St. Sth. HU9 33 F3
Crayford Clo. HU9 35 F1
Crescent St. HU6 11 H2
Cresswell Clo. HU2 32 B1
Creyke Clo. HU16 12 A4
Creyke La. HU15 25 E3
Crinan Dri. HU6 13 F2
Croft Dri. HU10 17 E5
Croft Vw,
  Kirk Ella. HU10 17 E5
Croft Vw,
  North Carr. HU7 21 E1
Crofters Dri. HU16 12 B5
*Crofton Av,
  Egton St. HU8 9 F1
Cromarty Clo. HU9 22 B5
Cromer St. HU5 20 A6
Cromwell Clo. HU3 32 A2
Cromwell Ct. HU10 17 F3
Cropton Rd. HU5 18 C3

*Crompton Villas,
  Estcourt St. HU9 33 F2
Cross St. HU1 8 B3
Crossall Hill La. HU15 25 F3
Crossfield Rd,
  Northfield. HU13 29 E2
Crossfield Rd,
  Anlaby Pk. HU4 30 C2
*Crossland Av,
  Holland St. HU9 33 F1
Crosswood Clo. HU7 14 D1
Crowland Clo. HU8 22 C1
Crowle St. HU9 33 F3
Crowther Way. HU14 26 D2
*Croyaland Av,
  Holland St. HU9 33 F1
Crusoe Ct. HU5 18 D3
Crystal St. HU3 19 H6
Cudworth Gro. HU3 33 E1
Cullen Clo. HU8 21 F3
Cumberland St. HU2 32 C1
*Cumberland Villas,
  Egton St. HU8 9 F1
Cumbrian Way. HU7 14 B1
Cundall Clo. HU3 33 G1
Curlew Clo. HU7 15 F6
Curzon St. HU3 19 E6
*Cuthbert Av,
  Airlie St. HU3 31 F2
Cyprus St. HU9 34 B2
Cyprus Wk. HU9 34 C2
Dagger La. HU1 8 D5
Dairycoates Av. HU3 31 F3
Dairycoates Rd. HU4 30 D4
Daisyfield Dri. HU11 22 D2
Dalby Gro. HU9 22 C5
Dale Clo. HU14 26 D2
Dale Rd,
  Elloughton. HU15 24 C2
Dale Rd,
  Swanland. HU14 26 C1
Dale Walk. HU15 25 E3
Dalesway. HU10 16 D4
Dalkeith Clo. HU7 14 D3
Dalsetter Rise. HU8 21 H2
Dalton St. HU8 21 D1
Daltry St. HU3 31 H3
Dalwood Clo. HU7 4 D5
Dam Green La. HU15 24 C1
Danby Clo. HU8 15 H6
Danepark Rd. HU6 12 D2
Danes Dri. HU13 29 E5
Dansom La. HU8 9 H2
Dansom La Nth. HU8 32 D1
Danthorpe Gro. HU8 22 A6
Danube Rd. HU5 18 B4
Darnholm Ct. HU8 21 G1
*Darrismere Villas,
  Edinburgh St. HU3 31 F2
Dart Gro. HU8 22 C2
Datchet Garth. HU4 29 G3
Davenport Av. HU13 28 D5
David Whitfield
  Clo. HU3 31 E2
Davids Clo. HU16 10 C1
Davidstow Clo. HU7 14 C6
Daville Clo. HU5 18 A4
Davis Clo. HU10 17 E3
Dawnay Dri. HU10 17 H5
Dawney Rd. HU11 33 G1
Day St. HU3 31 H1
Dayton Rd. HU5 18 C3
De la Pole Av. HU3 19 H3
Deal Clo. HU8 15 G6
Deans Dri. HU8 22 A3
Dearne Gro. HU8 33 E1
Deben Gro. HU8 22 C1
Dee St. HU3 31 G3
Deepdale Gro. HU9 33 G2
Deerhurst Gro. HU7 20 C1
*Delaware Av,
  De la Pole Av. HU3 19 E5
Delhi St. HU9 34 B2
Delius Clo. HU4 29 G1
Denaby Ct. HU8 33 E1
Dene Rd. HU16 11 G2
Dene St. HU9 33 F1
Denesway. HU13 28 D3
Denholme Av. HU6 13 G4
Denmark St. HU3 33 F3
Dent Rd. HU5 18 C1
Derby St. HU3 32 A1
Derringham Av. HU4 30 A1
Derrringham St. HU3 19 H5
Derrymore Rd. HU10 16 D1
Derwent Av. HU14 27 B8
*Derwent Av,
  Alfonso St. HU9 31 G2
Derwent Clo. HU16 12 C5
*Derwent Gro,
  Princes Rd.HU5 19 H3
Derwent St. HU8 21 E6
Desmond Av. HU6 13 H6
*Devon Gro,
  Sculcoates La. HU5 20 A6

Devon St. HU16 12 B4
*Devonport Av,
  Pretoria St. HU3 31 E1
*Devonshire Villas,
  Wellsted St. HU3 31 G2
Diadem Gro. HU9 22 D3
Dibsdane. HU6 12 D3
Didscourt. HU6 12 D4
Digby Garth. HU4 14 D4
Dingley Clo. HU6 13 G4
Ditmas Av. HU4 30 A1
Division Rd. HU3 31 G3
Dixon Ct. HU16 11 H4
Dock Office Row. HU1 9 E2
Dock St. HU1 8 D3
Dodswell Gro. HU9 35 E1
Dodthorpe. HU6 13 E2
Doncaster St. HU3 31 F1
Doongarth. HU4 29 G2
Dorado Clo. HU3 31 F2
Dorchester Rd. HU7 20 D2
*Doris Vale,
  Aylesford St. HU3 31 F2
Dorking Clo. HU8 22 B3
Dornoch Dri. HU8 21 E5
*Dorothy Gro,
  Newington St. HU3 31 E2
Dorset St. HU4 30 D4
Douglas Rd. HU8 22 D2
Dovedale Gro. HU9 33 G2
*Dover Cres,
  Folkestone St. HU5 20 A6
Dover St. HU3 19 H4
Dower Rise. HU14 26 E3
Downfield Av. HU6 13 F2
Downing Gro. HU9 34 A1
Downs Cres. HU5 18 C3
Drayton Clo. HU8 22 D3
Dressay Gro. HU8 21 H1
Driffield Clo. HU9 11 F3
Dringshaw. HU6 13 E3
Drovers Rise. HU15 24 B1
Drydales. HU10 16 D5
Dryden St. HU8 21 F6
Drypool Bri. HU1 9 F3
Drypool Way. HU9 33 E3
Duddon Gro. HU8 22 C2
Duesbery St. HU5 19 H4
Dulverton Clo. HU7 14 C4
*Dumbarton Av,
  Clyde St. HU3 31 E2
*Dunblane Clo,
  Stirling St. HU3 31 E1
Dundee St. HU5 19 E5
Dunkeld Dri. HU6 13 G2
Dunlin Clo.HU7 15 F6
Dunmow Clo. HU8 22 C2
Dunnock Clo. HU8 15 G6
Dunscombe Pk. HU8 21 E6
Dunston Rd. HU5 18 C6
Dunswell Clo. HU6 13 F4
Dunswell Rd. HU16 12 B1
Dunswell Rd. HU16 12 B4
Dunvegan Rd. HU8 21 H1
Durban St. HU8 9 G1
Durham St. HU8 33 E1
Durham Villas,
  Middleburg St. HU9 33 F1
Dyke Clo. HU13 29 E5
Eagle Ter. HU8 32 D2
Ealdane. HU6 12 D3
Ealing Clo. HU8 22 A3
Earles Rd. HU9 33 F3
Earlscourt. HU6 12 D4
Earsham Clo. HU8 22 C1
Easby Ct. HU5 18 B2
Easenby Av. HU10 16 D5
Easenby Clo. HU14 26 F2
Easethorpe. HU6 13 E2
East Carr Rd. HU8 21 H1
East Dale Rd. HU14 25 G4
East Ella Dri. HU4 30 B1
East Gro. HU3 30 C3
East Mnt. HU14 27 C7
East Park Av. HU8 21 G5
East St. HU9 9 G2
Eastbourne St. HU3 31 F2
*Eastern Villas,
  Brazil St. HU9 33 E2
*Eastern Villas,
  Holland St. HU9 33 F1
Eastfield Rd. HU4 30 C1
Eastmount Av. HU8 22 C3
Easton Av. HU8 20 B6
Eaton Clo. HU14 17 E2
Ebberston Gro. HU5 18 D2
Ebor Clo. HU8 22 C2
Ecclesfield Av. HU9 34 D1
*Eddlethorpe,
  Buckingham St. HU8 21 E6
Eden Dri. HU8 21 E5
*Eden Gro,
  Eastbourne St. HU3 31 F2
Eden Rise. HU10 17 E1
Edendale. HU7 20 C1

Edgar St. HU3 32 A5
Edgecumbe St. HU5 19 G2
Edgeware Av. HU9 33 H1
Edinburgh St. HU3 31 F2
Edison Gro. HU9 21 H6
Edith Cavell Ct. HU5 19 E1
*Edmonton Villas,
  Ceylon St. HU9 34 C3
Edward St. HU13 29 F4
Egginton Clo. HU10 17 E4
Egginton St. HU2 8 D2
Eglinton Av. HU9 22 A4
Egton St. HU8 9 F1
Egton Villas. HU8 9 G1
Egypt St. HU9 34 C2
*Elder Av,
  Abbey St. HU9 33 E2
Elderwood Ct. HU3 31 H2
Eldon Gro. HU5 20 A6
*Eldon Gro,
  Athol St. HU3 31 E2
*Eldon Gro.
  Goddard Av. HU5 19 G3
*Eldon Gro,
  Granville St. HU3 31 F1
Eleanor Ct. HU9 22 C5
Elgar Rd. HU3 30 A3
*Ella Gro,
  Mulgrave St. HU8 9 F1
Ella St. HU5 19 F3
*Ellens Villas,
  Holland St. HU9 33 F1
Ellerbeck Ct,
  More Hall Dri. HU8 21 G1
Ellerburn Av. HU6 13 E3
Ellerby Gro. HU9 22 A6
Ellerker Dri. HU10 17 E1
Ellerker Rise. HU10 16 D1
Ellesmere Av. HU8 22 A4
Ellingham Clo. HU3 22 C2
Ellis St. HU9 33 E2
Elloughton Clo. HU16 11 F3
Elloughton Dale. HU15 24 D1
Elloughton Gro. HU16 13 E6
Elloughton Rd. HU15 24 B4
Elm Av,
  Elloughton. HU15 24 C3
Elm Av,
  Garden Village. HU8 21 E6
*Elm Gro, De la
  Pole Av. HU3 19 E5
Elm St. HU5 19 H3
*Elm Ter,
  Queens Rd. HU5 19 H3
Elm Tree Ct. HU16 12 A5
*Elm Villas,
  Brazil St. HU9 33 E2
Elmbridge Par. HU6 35 E1
Elmfield. HU6 13 F5
Elmfield Dr. HU16 11 H3
Elms Dri. HU10 16 D3
Elmtree Av. HU14 27 B7
Elsham Rise. HU13 28 D4
*Elsie Villas,
  Holland St. HU9 33 F1
Elsiemere Wk. HU4 30 A1
*Elsternwick Av,
  Durham St. HU8 21 E6
Elston Clo. HU6 20 A2
Elsworth Ct. HU5 18 B3
Elveley Dri. HU10 16 B3
Elvington Clo. HU6 13 F4
Emberton Pk. HU7 14 C3
Emerald Gro. HU3 31 F3
Emmott Rd. HU8 13 G3
Emprimgham St. HU9 33 G2
Ena St. HU3 31 G1
Endike La. HU6 13 E5
Endsleigh St. HU3 19 E6
*Endsleigh Villas,
  Reynoldson St. HU5 19 G3
Endymion St. HU8 33 E1
England Rd. HU11 23 G1
English Clo. HU3 32 A5
English Gro. HU3 32 A6
Ennerdale Link Rd. HU6 13 F1
Ennerdale. HU7 14 A6
Enstone Garth. HU7 14 D4
Epping Clo. HU8 22 A2
Eppleworth Rd. HU16 11 E3
Epworth St. HU5 20 A6
*Erminston Villas,
  Rosmead St. HU9 33 F2
Ernest Kirkwood
  Clo. HU5 18 C4
*Ernest's Av,
  Holland St. HU9 33 F1
*Ernest's Villas,
  Holland St. HU9 33 F1
*Esk Cres,
  Worthing St. HU5 20 A4
Eskdale Av. HU9 33 H1
Esmond St. HU5 20 A6
Essex St. HU4 30 D4

Estcourt St. HU9 33 F2
*Estcourt Villas,
  Estcourt St. HU9 33 F2
*Esthers Av,
  Eastbourne St. HU3 31 F2
Etherington Dri. HU6 13 H6
Etherington Rd. HU6 13 H5
Eton St. HU3 31 G3
Etton Clo. HU16 11 F3
Etton Gro. HU6 12 D5
Euston Clo. HU3 31 H2
*Evas Av, De la
  Pole Av. HU3 19 E5
Evergreen Dri. HU6 13 G2
Everingham Wk. HU5 18 B3
Everthorpe Clo. HU3 31 H2
Exchange St. HU5 20 B6
Exeter Gro. HU9 22 C6
Exeter St. HU16 12 B4
Exmouth St. HU5 19 G2
Exton Clo. HU7 14 C4
*Faceby Wk,
  Bowes Wk. HU5 18 D2
Fairbourne Clo. HU7 14 C1
Faircourt. HU6 12 D4
Fairfax Av. HU5 19 E1
Fairfield Av. HU10 16 D2
Fairfield Rd. HU5 18 D1
*Fairmount Av,
  De la Pole Av. HU3 19 E5
Falcon Clo. HU4 30 C5
Falkirk Clo. HU7 14 D1
Falkland St. HU8 35 E1
Falmouth St. HU5 19 G2
Falsgrave Clo. HU5 18 C5
Far Bell Pl. HU9 22 D6
Faraday St. HU9 21 G6
Farlington Clo. HU9 22 D3
Farndale Av. HU9 33 G1
Farnella Clo. HU3 31 F2
Farnley Sq. HU5 19 G3
Faroes Clo. HU5 22 B4
Farrington St. HU5 20 B6
*Farringdon Vw,
  Farringdon St. HU5 20 B6
Faversham Av. HU4 30 A1
Fawcett Clo. HU3 19 H4
Fawley Clo. HU5 20 A5
Felbridge Clo. HU5 23 E6
Feldane. HU6 12 D2
Fenby Ct. HU13 29 F3
Fenchurch St. HU5 20 A6
Ferens Av. HU6 19 G1
*Ferens Villas,
  Rosmead St. HU9 33 F2
Ferens Ct. HU9 33 F2
Ferens Gdns. HU16 11 G1
Ferensway. HU1 8 B2
*Fern Av,
  Middleburg St. HU9 35 E5
Fern Clo. HU2 32 B2
*Fern Dale,
  Lambert St. HU5 19 H3
*Fern Dale,
  Sherburn St. HU9 33 F1
*Fern Gro,
  Folkestone St. HU5 20 A6
*Fern Gro,
  Perth St. HU5 19 F5
Ferndale. HU8 9 G1
Ferndale Av. HU10 17 E2
*Ferndale Av,
  Exmouth St. HU5 19 G2
Fernhill Rd. HU5 18 D1
Fernland Ct. HU15 24 C4
Ferriby Ct. HU5 24 A4
Ferriby Gro. HU6 13 E6
Ferriby High Rd. HU14 27 C6
Ferriby La. HU13 28 C4
Ferries St. HU9 33 G3
Ferry La. HU6 20 C4
Ferry Rd. HU13 29 E4
Field St. HU9 9 H1
Fieldside Garth. HU6 13 G2
*Filey Gro,
  Rhodes St. HU3 31 G2
Fimber Av. HU16 11 H4
*Finch Croft,
  Linnet Dri. HU8 21 G1
Finchley Clo. HU8 22 A2
Finkle St,
  Cottingham. HU16 11 H2
Finkle St, Hull. HU1 8 D6
Finningley Garth. HU7 15 E4
Finsbury Gro. HU2 32 B2
First La, Anlaby. HU10 17 G5
First La,
  Northfield. HU13 29 G2
Fish St. HU1 8 D5
Fishemore Av. HU13 29 F4
Fisher Clo. HU10 17 F1
Fishermans Way. HU3 31 H3
Fishwick Av. HU3 29 E4
Fitzroy St. HU5 20 A6
Flaxdale Ct. HU5 18 C4

Flaxton Rd. HU5 18 C3
Fleet Ct. HU5 20 B6
Fleming Wk. HU4 30 C5
Flemingdale. HU7 20 C1
Fletcher Ct. HU13 29 E3
Flinton Gro. HU9 34 B1
Flinton St. HU3 31 F3
*Floral Av,
  Rensburg St. HU9 33 F1
*Floral Av,
  Seymour St. HU3 31 E3
Florence Av. HU13 29 F4
*Florence Av,
  Cadogan St. HU3 31 G2
*Florence Av,
  Queens Rd. HU5 19 H3
*Florence Gro,
  Lorraine St. HU8 20 D5
*Folkestone Av,
  Folkestone St. HU5 20 A6
Folkestone St. HU5 20 A6
Folkton Av. HU16 11 G4
Forber Av. HU9 22 D6
Forbes Av. HU6 13 G3
Foredyke Av. HU7 20 D4
Forester Way. HU4 30 C4
Formby Clo. HU16 12 C5
Fortune Clo. HU8 21 H3
Forty Acres. HU10 17 G4
Forty Steps. HU10 17 G4
Foss Gro. HU8 22 C2
Fossdale Clo. HU8 21 G1
Foster St. HU5 20 C6
Foston Gro. HU9 34 B1
Fountain Clo. HU13 28 C2
Fountain Rd. HU2 32 A1
Fountain St. HU3 33 A4
Four Acre Clo. HU10 16 D5
Foxhill Clo. HU9 23 E5
Foxholme Rd. HU7 15 F6
Foynes Grn. HU8 22 C3
Fraisethorpe. HU6 13 E2
Frampton Clo. HU7 20 D2
*Frances Av,
  Wellsted St. HU3 31 G2
Francis St. HU2 8 C2
Frank Hill Ct. HU5 19 F3
*Franklin Av,
  Franklin St. HU9 33 E2
Franklin St. HU9 33 E2
*Franklin Villas,
  Mulgrave St. HU8 9 F1
Freehold St. HU3 32 A2
Freeman Av. HU5 24 C4
Freemantle Av. HU9 22 D6
Freetown Ct. HU6 13 F5
Freetown Way. HU2 8 B2
Freightliner Rd. HU3 31 E5
Freightlinger Way. HU3 31 E4
Frodsham St. HU8 34 B2
Frog Hall La. HU7 20 C2
Frome Rd. HU8 22 C1
Fulford Cres. HU10 17 H3
Fulmar Clo. HU7 15 F6
Furness. HU7 14 D1
Gainford Gro. HU9 23 E6
Galfrid Rd. HU11 23 F1
Gallard Clo. HU3 31 F3
Ganstead Gro. HU9 22 A6
Ganstead La. HU11 23 E1
Ganton Av. HU16 11 H4
Ganton Way. HU10 17 G3
Garfield Clo. HU5 35 E1
*Garholme Villas,
  Rensburg St. HU9 33 F1
Garland Clo. HU9 22 D3
Garnet Gro. HU3 31 F3
Garrick Clo. HU8 21 H3
Garrison Rd. HU1 9 E5
Garrowby Wk. HU5 18 B3
Garth Av. HU11 23 G1
Garton Gro. HU5 18 B5
*Gascoigne Ct,
  De Grey St. HU5 19 H5
Gatwick Garth. HU7 15 E4
Gee St. HU3 31 G2
Gemsbok Clo. HU4 30 C5
Geneva Way. HU7 21 E3
George St,
  Cottingham. HU16 11 H2
George St, Hull. HU1 8 D3
George Yd. HU1 9 F4
*Georges Ct,
  Springburn St. HU3 31 E2
Gershwin Av. HU4 30 A3
Gibson La. HU14 25 G4
Gibson St. HU2 32 B2
Gifford Clo. HU7 14 C2
*Gilbert Av,
  Haltemprice St. HU3 31 E2
Gildane. HU6 12 D3
Gillamoor Clo. HU8 21 G1
Gillett St. HU3 31 F
Gillshill Rd. HU8 21 H
Gisburn Rd. HU13 29 F

Kinderscout Clo. HU7 14 C2
King Charles Clo. HU10 17 F4
King Edward St. HU1 8 C3
King Edwards Ter. HU15 24 A4
King St, Cottingham. HU16 12 A4
King St, Hull. HU1 8 D5
Kingfisher Clo. HU7 15 F6
Kingfisher Rise. HU7 21 G2
Kings Bench St. HU3 31 G2
Kings Cross Clo. HU3 12 A4
Kings Ct. HU16 12 A4
Kings Gdns. HU5 19 G3
Kingsbury Way. HU7 14 B3
Kingscott Clo. HU7 14 B5
*Kingsleigh, Bean St. HU3 31 H1
Kingsley Av. HU9 21 H5
Kingsley Clo. HU5 24 B5
Kingsport Clo. HU3 19 F5
Kingston Av. HU13 29 F4
Kingston Rise. HU10 17 E2
Kingston Road. HU10 17 E2
Kingston Sq. HU2 8 D2
Kingston St. HU1 8 B6
*Kingston Villas, Estcourt St. HU9 33 F2
Kingston Way. HU7 20 B3
Kingston Wharf. HU1 8 C6
Kingsway. HU16 12 A6
Kingtree Av. HU13 12 A5
Kinloss Garth. HU7 15 E5
Kinthorpe. HU6 13 F3
Kipling Wk. HU4 30 C5
Kiplington Clo. HU3 19 E6
Kirby Dri. HU16 12 A4
Kirk Clo. HU7 21 G2
Kirk Croft. HU16 11 H3
Kirk Rise. HU10 16 D4
Kirkby St. HU2 32 C2
*Kirkdale Gdns, Exmouth St. HU5 19 G2
Kirkham Clo. HU13 29 F3
Kirkham Dri. HU5 19 F4
Kirklands HU5 18 D4
*Kirkstead Av, Kirkstead St. HU8 20 D6
Kirkstead St. HU8 20 D6
Kirkstone Rd. HU5 18 C3
Kirkway. HU10 16 D4
Knapton Clo. HU6 18 D2
Knightscourt. HU6 12 D4
Knowles Av. HU16 13 G3
Knowsley Av. HU16 11 H2
Kyffin Av. HU9 22 D6
Kyle Clo. HU8 22 C2
*LB Avenue, Clyde St. HU8 31 E2
Laburnum Av. HU8 21 E5
*Laburnum Av, Hardy St. HU5 19 H2
Laburnum Ct. HU13 29 E4
Laburnum Dri. HU8 18 A6
*Laburnum Gro, Lorraine St. HU8 20 D5
Ladybower Clo. HU8 21 G1
Ladyside Clo. HU7 14 D3
Ladysmith Rd. HU10 17 F2
Ladywell Gate. HU15 25 E3
Lagoon Dri. HU7 15 F6
Lake Dri. HU7 21 H5
Lakeside Gro. HU4 30 C3
Lambert Av. HU15 24 C3
Lambert St. HU5 19 H2
Lambton St. HU5 19 G2
Lambwath Rd. HU8 21 F4
Lamorna Av. HU8 21 E5
Lanark St. HU5 19 F5
Lancaster Dri. HU8 21 F3
Land of Green Ginger. HU1 9 E4
Langdale Av. HU5 18 D3
Langdale Cres. HU16 11 G3
Langford Wk. HU4 18 A5
Langley Pk. HU7 14 C3
Langsett Rd. HU8 21 G1
Langtoft Gro. HU6 13 E5
Langtree Clo. HU7 14 C6
Lansdowne St. HU3 31 H1
Lanyon Clo. HU7 21 F1
Lapwing Clo. HU7 15 G6
Larard Av. HU6 13 H3
Larch Clo. HU5 19 H3
Larchmont Clo. HU15 24 B3
Larne Rd. HU7 14 B5
Lashbrook Garth. HU4 29 H1
Lastingham Clo. HU6 12 D4
*Laurel Av, Perth St. HU5 19 F5
Laurel Clo. HU5 18 B5
*Laurel Gro, Perry St. HU3 31 F1
*Laurel Villas, Estcourt St. HU9 33 F2
Lavender Wk. HU5 18 B5
Lawnsgarth. HU16 11 H1
Lawnswood. HU13 28 D3
Lawnswood Clo. HU7 21 F3
Lawrence Av. HU8 21 H4
Lawson Av. HU8 12 A4
Lawsons Clo. HU6 13 G5
Laxthorpe. HU6 13 F3
Laxton Garth. HU10 16 C2
Lea Cres. HU16 11 H3
Leads Rd. HU7 20 D3
Lealholm Ct. HU8 21 G1
*Leame Clo, Pulman St. HU3 19 E5
Leander Rd. HU9 22 C5
Leconfield Av. HU9 35 E1
Ledbury Rd. HU5 18 B2
Lee St. HU8 21 F5
Lee Smith St. HU3 33 G3
Leeming Garth. HU7 15 E5
Lees Wk. HU3 19 F6
Legard Dri. HU10 16 D4
Legarde Av. HU4 30 B1
Leicester St. HU3 32 A1
Leitholme Clo. HU7 14 D1
Leningrad Rd. HU7 20 C2
Leonard St. HU3 19 H5
*Leonards Av, Alexandra Rd. HU5 20 A5
*Leonards Av, Rhodes St. HU5 31 E2
*Leslie Gro, Lorraine St. HU8 20 D5
*Leura Gro, Tyne St. HU3 31 F3
Levin Gro. HU9 22 B6
Levisham Clo. HU6 12 D5
Levita Av. HU9 22 B6
Lexington Dri. HU4 30 B2
Leyburn Av. HU5 12 D6
*Leyland, New Bridge Rd. HU9 33 F2
Liberty La. HU1 9 E5
Liddell St. HU2 8 B1
*Lilac Av, Hardy St. HU5 19 H2
Lilac Av, Willerby. HU10 17 E2
*Lilac Av, Garden Village. HU8 21 E6
*Lily Gro, Greek St. HU3 31 E2
Lime Av. HU10 17 F2
Lime St. HU8 9 E1
Lime Tree Av. HU8 21 E6
Lime Tree La. HU11 23 F2
Limedane. HU6 13 E3
Limerick Clo. HU8 22 C2
Limetree Av. HU7 21 F2
Lincoln Grn. HU4 18 B6
Lincoln St. HU2 32 C2
Linden Av. HU16 12 B3
*Linden Gro, Folkestone St. HU5 20 A6
Lindengate Av. HU7 21 E3
Lindengate Way. HU7 21 E3
*Lindern Gro, Greek St. HU3 31 E2
Lindsey Pl. HU4 30 C1
Lingcourt. HU6 12 D4
Lingdale Rd. HU9 23 E5
Link Rd. HU16 12 A5
Linkfield Rd. HU5 18 D1
Linnaeus St. HU3 31 H1
Linnet Dri. HU8 15 G6
Linthorpe Gro. HU10 17 F3
Lismore Av. HU8 22 B5
Lisset Gro. HU6 13 G4
Lister St. HU3 32 A5
Litchfield Clo. HU2 32 B1
Little Mason St. HU2 9 E2
Little Queen St. HU1 8 C4
Little Reed St. HU2 8 C3
Little Weighton Rd. HU16 10 A1
Littlebeck Clo. HU3 19 F6
Littlefair Rd. HU9 34 B3
Littleham Clo. HU7 15 E6
Littondale. HU7 20 B1
Littondale. HU7 20 C1
Liverpool St. HU3 31 H1
Livingstone Rd. HU13 29 E5
*Lizzies Av, Rhodes St. HU3 31 E2
Loatley Grn. HU16 12 B5
Lockton Gro. HU6 18 C5
Lockwood St. HU2 8 D1
Lodge Clo. HU13 29 F4
Lodge Gro. HU9 21 G6
Lodge St. HU9 23 E5
Logan Clo. HU7 21 E1
Lombard St. HU2 8 A3
Lombardy Clo. HU5 18 B5
Lomond Rd. HU5 18 C4
Londesborough St. HU3 19 H6
Longden St. HU3 19 F6
Longford Gro. HU9 23 E6
Lonsdale St. HU3 31 F1
Lorne Clo. HU2 32 B2
Lorraine St. HU8 20 D5
*Lorrel Gro, Ruskin St. HU3 31 F1
Lothian Way. HU7 14 C2
*Louis Cres, Albemarle St. HU3 31 F2
Louis Dri. HU3 18 A5
Louis St. HU3 19 H5
Lovat Clo. HU3 8 A6
Loveridge Av. HU5 19 F3
Low Common La. HU15 25 E6
Low St. HU14 27 B7
Lowdale Clo. HU3 18 D4
Lowfield La. HU14 25 F4
Lowfield Rd. HU10 17 F5
Lowgate, Hull. HU1 9 E3
Lowgate, Sutton Ings. HU7 21 G2
Lowland Clo. HU7 15 F6
Lowther St. HU3 19 F6
Loxley Grn. HU4 18 A6
Loyd St. HU10 17 G5
Lulworth Av. HU3 29 G2
Lund Av. HU16 11 F3
Lunedale Clo. HU8 21 H1
Luton Rd. HU5 18 D5
Lyme Tree Av. HU13 29 F4
Lymington Garth. HU4 29 G2
Lyndhurst Av. HU6 12 C5
Lyngarth Av. HU16 12 B5
Lynmouth Clo. HU7 14 D4
*Lynslade Cres, Perth St. HU5 19 F5
Lynton Av, Northfield. HU4 29 H2
Lynton Av, Stepney. HU5 19 F4
*Lynton Av, Perth St West. HU5 19 F5
Lynwood Av. HU10 17 F5
*Lynwood Gro, Goddard Av. HU5 19 G3
Lyric Clo. HU3 31 H2
Lytham Dri. HU16 12 C5
Lythe Av. HU5 18 C1
*Mabels Av, Franklin St. HU8 33 E2
*Mables Villas, Holland St. HU3 33 F1
Machell St. HU2 9 E1
McKinley Av, Albemarle St. HU3 31 F2
*Macon Av, Minton St. HU5 20 A4
Madeley St. HU3 31 H3
Madison Gdns. HU5 19 F4
*Madoline Gro, Estcourt St. HU9 33 F2
Madron Clo. HU7 15 E6
*Mafeking Gro, Seymour St. HU5 31 E2
Main Rd. HU11 23 E2
Main St, Elloughton. HU15 24 C2
Main St, Hull. HU2 32 C1
Main St, Skidby. HU16 10 B2
Main St, Swanland. HU14 26 D3
Main St, Willerby. HU10 16 D1
Majestic St. HU9 22 A5
Maldon Dri. HU9 33 E4
Malham Av. HU4 30 B1
Mallard Rd. HU9 22 C4
Mallyan Clo. HU8 21 G1
Malm St. HU3 31 G1
Malmo Rd. HU7 20 A2
Malpas Clo. HU7 14 C4
Malton Clo. HU9 9 G2
Malvern Av. HU5 19 G3
*Malvern Av, Cecil St. HU3 31 E2
Malvern Cres. HU5 18 C3
Malvern Rd. HU5 18 C3
Manchester St. HU3 31 F3
Mancklin Av. HU8 21 F3
Manet Av. HU8 33 F1
Manor Ct. HU10 16 B4
Manor Dri. HU15 24 C2
Manor Fields. HU10 16 B4
Manor House St. HU1 8 C6
Manor Rd, East Ella. HU5 18 B5
Manor Rd, Swanland. HU14 26 D3
Manor St. HU1 9 E4
Manor Way. HU10 17 G5
Mansfield Pk. HU5 19 F5
Manston Garth. HU7 15 E5
Manvers St. HU5 19 G3
Maple Av. HU10 17 G3
Maple Clo. HU5 18 B5
Maple Gro. HU8 21 F6
Maple St. HU5 19 H3
Mapleleaf Ct. HU16 11 G4
Maplewood Av. HU8 18 A6
Mappleton Gro. HU9 22 B6
*Mareham Av, Ena St. HU3 31 G1
Marfleet Av. HU9 34 C3
Marfleet La, Marfleet. HU9 34 C2
Marfleet La, Sutton Ings. HU9 22 B4
Margaret Gro. HU13 29 F4
Margaret St. HU3 32 A1
Mariene Wharf. HU1 8 C6
Marina Ct. HU1 8 D5
Marine Av. HU14 27 B8
Market Grn. HU16 12 A5
Market Pl. HU1 8 D5
Market Sq. HU1 8 D5
Marlborough Av. HU5 19 F4
Marlborough Ter. HU2 8 B2
Marlowe St. HU8 21 F5
*Marlsborough Av. HU13 28 D4
Marmaduke St. HU3 31 G3
Marne St. HU5 19 F4
Marsdale. HU7 20 C1
Marsden Landing. HU6 13 H3
Marshall Av. HU10 17 F3
Marshall St. HU5 19 G3
Marshington Clo. HU16 19 E6
*Marske Wk, Bishop Alcock Rd. HU5 18 C2
Marton Gro. HU6 13 E6
Marvel St. HU9 9 H3
Marydene Dri. HU6 13 H6
Mason St, Princess St. HU2 9 E2
Mason St, Worship St. HU2 8 D2
Massey Clo. HU3 31 F2
Massey St. HU3 31 F3
*Matlock Villas, Estcourt St. HU9 33 F2
Maurice Av. HU8 20 D6
Maxim Clo. HU3 31 H2
Maxwell St. HU5 20 C5
May Gro. HU13 28 D3
May St. HU5 20 A5
*May Ter, May St. HU5 20 A5
May Tree Av. HU8 21 E6
Maybury Rd. HU9 22 A5
*Maye Gro, Danson La Nth. HU8 32 D1
*Maye Gro, Egdon St. HU8 9 F1
*Maye Gro, Perth St West. HU5 19 F5
*Maye Gro, Sculcoates La. HU5 20 A6
Mayfair Ct. HU5 19 H2
Mayfield St. HU3 19 H5
*Mayfield Villas, Rosmead St. HU9 33 F2
Mayland Av. HU5 17 H3
Mayland Dri. HU5 17 H3
Maythorpe Clo. HU3 19 E5
Mayville Av. HU8 20 D5
Mead St. HU8 21 G3
Mead Walk. HU4 30 B1
Meadow Garth. HU6 13 G2
*Meadow Vale, Estcourt St. HU9 33 F2
Meadow Wk. HU14 26 D2
Meadow Way. HU16 11 G4
Meadowbank Rd. HU3 30 D1
Medina Rd. HU8 22 D2
Melbourne St. HU5 19 H2
*Melrose Cres, Greek St. HU3 31 E1
Melrose St. HU3 31 E1
*Melrose Villas, Chestnut Av. HU5 19 H3
Melton Bottom. HU14 25 G4
Melton Fields. HU14 25 H5
Melton Old Rd. HU14 25 G4
Melton Rd. HU14 27 A6
Meltonby Av. HU8 18 B3
Melville St. HU1 8 B5
Melwood Gro. HU16 20 A6
Mendip Clo. HU3 31 H2
Mere Way. HU14 26 D3
Merlin Clo. HU8. 15 G6
Merrick St. HU9 9 H3
Mersey St. HU8 33 E1
*Mersey Villas, Rosmead St. HU9 33 F2
Merton Gro. HU9 34 A1
Michams Ct. HU8 22 A3
Mickley Gro. HU3 22 D6
Middle Dike La. HU16 12 C3
Middleburg St. HU9 33 F1
Middleham Clo. HU9 33 G2
Middlesex Rd. HU8 22 A3
*Middleston Av, Rensburg St. HU9 33 F1
Middleton St. HU3 19 H5
*Middleton Villas, Clyde St. HU3 31 E2
Midgley Clo. HU3 31 H2
Midland St. HU1 8 B5
Midmere Av. HU7 21 E1
Midway Gro. HU4 30 C3
Milford Gro. HU9 35 E1
Mill Beck La. HU16 12 A3
Mill La, Cottingham. HU16 11 F2
Mill La, Kirk Ella. HU10 16 D4
Mill La, Elloughton. HU15 24 B2
Mill La West. HU15 24 A3
Mill Rise, Skidby. HU16 10 C1
Mill Rise, Swanland. HU14 26 C3
Mill Road, Skidby. HU16 10 D1
Mill Road, Swanland. HU14 26 A3
Mill St. HU1 8 B3
Mill Wk. HU16 12 B5
Milldane. HU6 12 D3
Millers Wk. HU5 19 E2
Millhouse Woods La. HU16 12 A3
Millport Dri. HU4 29 H3
Milne Rd. HU5 22 C4
Minehead Rd. HU7 14 D5
Minerva Ter. HU1 8 D6
Minnies Gro. HU4 19 F6
*Minnies Gro, Beilby St. HU3 31 E2
Minster Clo. HU8 21 G3
Minton St. HU5 20 A4
Mirfield Gro. HU9 22 C6
Mitcham Rd. HU8 22 A3
Mizzen Rd. HU6 13 G3
Moffat Clo. HU8 21 F4
Mollison Rd. HU4 29 G2
Monic Av. HU13 29 F2
Monkton Clo. HU16 11 G4
Monkton Wk. HU8 22 D2
Monmouth St. HU4 30 D4
Mons St. HU5 19 F5
Montcalm Wk. HU16 11 G4
*Montreal Av, Albemarle St. HU3 31 F2
Montreal Cres. HU16 11 F4
*Montrose Av, Montrose St. HU8 31 D1
*Montrose Av, Seymour St. HU5 31 E2
Montrose St. HU8 32 D1
Moor Grn. HU4 18 B6
Moorbeck Clo. HU6 18 D1
Moorfoot Clo. HU7 14 D2
Moorhouse Rd. HU5 18 A4
More Hall Dri. HU8 21 G1
Moreton Bay. HU11 23 E2
Morley St. HU5 20 C5
Morpeth St. HU3 19 H5
Morrill St. HU9 33 F1
Morrison Av. HU6 13 G3
Mortimer Av. HU10 17 G5
Mortlake Clo. HU5 21 G3
Morton St. HU3 19 H6
Moseley Hill. HU11 23 E2
Motherwell Clo. HU8 21 F3
Mount Av. HU13 29 E5
Mount Pleasant. HU8 32 D1
Mount Vernon. HU11 23 E2
Mount Vw. HU14 27 B5
Moy Ct. HU8 13 E5
Muirfield Pk. HU5 19 F4
Mulberry Clo. HU9 34 C1
Mulcourt. HU8 12 D4
Mulgrave St. HU8 9 F1
Mullion Clo. HU7 21 E1
Munroe Clo. HU7 21 F4
Murray Cres. HU16 11 G4
Murrayfield Rd. HU5 19 E2
Muston Av. HU16 11 G3
Muston Gro. HU7 23 E4
*Myrtle Av, Wellsted St. HU3 31 G1
*Myrtle Av, Williamson St. HU9 9 H1
*Myrtle Gro, Lorraine St. HU8 20 D5
*Myrtle Gro, Springburn St. HU3 31 E2
Myton Bri. HU1 9 F5
Myton St. HU1 8 C5
Mytongate. HU1 8 B5
Naburn St. HU3 31 F1
Nairn Clo. HU6 13 F3
Nalton Clo. HU6 12 A4
Nandyke Clo. HU10 17 C2
Narrow La. HU14 27 E5
Narvik St. HU7 20 E5

Nashcourt. HU6 12 D4
National Av. HU5 19 E3
Navenby Gro. HU7 14 C3
Naylors Row. HU7 9 H2
Neasden Clo. HU8 21 G3
Neat Marsh Rd. HU12 35 F2
Neatshead Garth. HU7 15 F5
Nectan Clo. HU3 31 F3
Nelson Rd. HU5 18 A5
Nelson St. HU1 9 E6
*Nelson Villas,
  Egton St. HU8 9 F1
*Nepean Gro,
  Tyne St. HU3 31 F3
Neptune St. HU3 32 A6
Nesfield Av,
  Perth St West, HU5 19 F5
Nester Gro. HU9 22 D3
Netherton Rd. HU4 29 H1
Neville Clo. HU3 8 A6
New Bridge Rd. HU3 8 A4
New Cleveland St. HU8 9 F1
New Cross St. HU1 8 D4
New Finkle St. HU1 11 H2
New Garden St. HU1 8 D3
New George St. HU1 8 D1
New Michael St. HU1 8 B5
New St. HU3 31 E2
New Village Rd. HU14 12 B4
Newbald Gro. HU6 12 D5
Newcomen St. HU9 21 G6
Newgate St. HU1 12 A5
Newholme Clo. HU6 13 E5
Newington Av. HU4 30 C2
Newington St. HU3 31 E3
Newland Av. HU5 19 H3
*Newland Ct,
  Alexandra Rd. HU9 19 H2
Newland Gro. HU5 19 H2
Newland Pk. HU5 19 F1
Newlands Pk Av.HU6 19 G1
Newlyn Clo,
  Northfield. HU13 29 G3
Newlyn Clo,
  Sutton-on-Hull. HU7 21 E1
Newport Clo. HU3 31 H1
Newsham Garth.HU4 30 A2
*Newstead Av,
  Newstead St. HU5 19 F5
Newstead St. HU5 19 F5
Newton St. HU3 31 G3
*Newton Villas,
  Estcourt St. HU9 33 F2
Newtondale. HU7 20 C1
Newtown Sq. HU3 33 G3
Nicholson Clo. HU16 11 H2
Nicholson St. HU3 20 B6
Nidderdale. HU7 20 B1
Nith Gro. HU8 22 D1
Nithdale Gdns. HU5 20 B6
Noddle Hill Way. HU7 14 D4
Nordale Clo. HU8 21 G1
Norfolk St. HU2 8 B1
Normanton Rise. HU4 18 B6
Nornabell St. HU8 33 E1
North Bri. HU1 9 F2
North Church Side. HU1 9 E5
North Country Ct. HU9 33 H1
North Dri,
  Swanland. HU4 26 E3
North Moor La. HU16 12 B3
North Rd. HU4 30 D1
North St, Anlaby. HU10 17 F4
North St, Hull. HU2 8 B3
North Walls. HU1 9 F3
Northcroft Dri. HU8 21 G1
Northdale Pk. HU14 26 E2
Northella Dri. HU4 30 D1
Northfield. HU14 26 D2
Northfield Av. HU13 29 E3
Northfield Rd. HU3 31 E1
*Northfield Villas,
  Rosmead St.HU9 33 F2
Northgate,
  Cottingham. HU16 12 A4
Northgate,
  Northfield. HU13 29 E3
Northgate Pl. HU13 29 E3
Northolme Circle. HU13 29 E3
Northolme Cres. HU13 29 E3
Northolme Rd. HU13 29 E3
Northolt Clo. HU8 21 G2
Northstead Dri.HU10 17 F1
Northumberland
  Av. HU2 32 B1
Northwood Clo. HU8 22 B1
Norton Gro. HU4 30 C3
Norwood Clo. HU4 17 F4
Novello Garth. HU4 30 A3
Nunburnholme
  Av. HU14 27 B7
Nunburnholme Pk. HU5 18 B6
Nunnington Clo. HU5 19 G3

Nursery Ct. HU15 24 C4
Nursery Wk. HU16 12 C5
*Oak Av,
  De la Pole Av. HU3 19 E5
Oak Av,
  Elloughton. HU15 24 C3
Oak Av, Willerby. HU10 17 E2
Oak Dri. HU8 18 A6
Oakdene. HU16 12 A5
Oakingdon Garth. HU7 15 F5
*Oakland Villas,
  Reynoldson St. HU5 19 G3
Oaklands Dri,
  Northfield. HU13 29 E3
Oaklands Dri,
  Willerby. HU10 16 D2
Oaktree Dri. HU8 21 F1
Oakwell Gro. HU8 33 E1
Oakwood Clo. HU5 18 A6
*Oban Av,
  De la Pole Av. HU3 31 H2
Oban Av. HU3 22 B5
Occupation La. HU14 26 E1
Ocean Blvd. HU9 9 G5
Old Annandale
  Rd. HU10 16 D3
Oldfield Av. HU6 13 G5
Oldstead Av. HU6 13 E5
Oliver Ct. HU4 30 D4
Ombwell Gro. HU8 33 E1
On Hill. HU14 26 E3
Onyx Gro. HU3 31 F3
Orchard Clo. HU10 17 G4
Orchard Cft. HU16 12 B3
Orchard Dri. HU13 29 E4
Orchard Park Rd. HU6 13 E3
Orchard Rd,
  Skidby. HU16 10 B1
Orchard Rd,
  Anlaby Pk. HU4 30 A2
Oriel Gro. HU9 34 B1
Orion Clo.HU3 31 F2
Orkney Clo. HU3 21 G1
Ormerod Cres. HU5 18 C3
Ormerod Rd. HU5 18 C3
Ormesby Wk. HU5 18 C1
*Ormington Villas,
  Field St. HU9 9 H1
Ormonde Av. HU6 20 A3
*Ormonde Villas,
  Wynburg St. HU9 33 F1
Orniscourt. HU6 12 D3
*Orpington Villas,
  Rensburg St. HU9 33 F1
Osborne St. HU1 8 B5
Oslo Rd. HU7 20 B2
Osprey Clo. HU6 13 F2
Otley Clo. HU9 22 C6
Otterburn St. HU3 31 E2
Ottowa Clo. HU16 11 G4
Outlands Rd. HU16 12 C6
Outram Clo. HU2 32 B2
Overland Rd. HU16 12 B5
Overstand Dri. HU7 21 F2
Overton Av. HU10 17 F2
*Owthorne Villas,
  Rosmead St. HU9 33 F2
Oxenhope Rd. HU6 13 H3
Oxford St. HU2 32 C1
Packman La. HU10 16 C2
Padstow Clo. HU7 14 B4
Paisley St. HU3 19 F6
Palmcourt. HU6 12 D3
Palmer Av. HU10 17 F3
Paragon St. HU1 8 B4
Park Av,
  Cottingham. HU16 11 H2
Park Av,
  Northfield. HU13 29 E3
Park Av, Stepney. HU5 19 F4
Park Av West. HU5 19 F4
*Park Av, Perry St. HU3 31 F1
Park Gro. HU5 19 H4
*Park Gro,
  Wynburg St. HU9 33 F1
Park La,
  Cottingham. HU16 11 G1
Park La, Stepney. HU5 32 A1
Park La E. HU4 30 B1
Park La W. HU4 30 B1
Park Rd, Stepney. HU5 32 A1
Park Rd, Welton. HU15 25 E3
Park Row. HU1 32 A3
Park St. HU3 8 A4
Park Vw,
  Gipsyville. HU4 30 D3
Park Vw, Hull. HU3 19 F6
Park Wk,
  Anlaby Pk. HU4 30 A2
Park Wk,
  Sutton-on-Hull. HU7 21 F1
Parkfield Av. HU14 27 B7
Parkfield Dri. HU3 31 E1

Parkhurst Clo. HU8 22 D2
Parklands Cres. HU14 27 B6
Parklands Dri. HU14 27 B6
Parkside Clo,
  Cottingham. HU16 11 G2
Parkside Clo,
  Stepney. HU5 19 G4
Parkstone Rd. HU6 13 H4
Parliament St,
  Welton. HU15 25 E3
Parliament St, Hull. HU1 8 D4
Parthian Rd. HU9 22 C5
Patrington Garth. HU7 15 F6
Patterdale Rd. HU5 18 D5
Paull Rd. HU12 35 H4
Pavilion Clo. HU8 21 E5
*Pavilion Cres,
  Worthing St. HU5 20 A5
Paxdale. HU7 14 B6
Peacehaven Clo. HU7 20 C7
*Peach Tree Ct,
  Cavill Pl. HU3 31 H2
Pear Tree Clo. HU8 21 F4
Pearson Av. HU5 20 A6
Pearson St. HU2 8 A2
Pease St. HU3 8 A4
Peasholme. HU13 28 C4
Peckham Clo. HU8 21 G3
Peel St. HU3 19 H5
Peggy Farrow La. HU15 24 C1
Pelham Dri. HU9 33 E2
*Pemberton Gdns,
  Folkestone St. HU5 20 A6
Pemberton St. HU8 9 G1
Pembroke Gro. HU9 34 A1
*Pembroke Villas,
  Rosmead St. HU9 33 F2
Pendeen Gro. HU8 20 D5
Pendle Clo. HU7 14 C3
Pendrill St. HU5 32 A1
Penistone Clo. HU9 33 F2
Pennine Way. HU7 14 C2
Pennington St. HU8 9 G1
Pennyson Av. HU5 19 F4
Penrose Clo. HU7 14 C5
Penshurst Av. HU9 29 F2
Pentland Clo. HU8 21 H1
Penwith Dri. HU10 17 G4
Peppleton Clo. HU7 21 E4
Percy St. HU2 8 C3
Peregrine Clo. HU4 30 C5
Perivale Clo. HU8 22 B3
Perran Clo. HU7 21 E1
Perry St. HU3 31 F1
Perth St. HU5 19 F5
Perth St West. HU5 19 E5
Petersfield Clo. HU7 20 D1
Petersham Clo. HU8 22 B3
Petuaria Clo. HU5 24 B4
Pevensey Clo. HU7 20 D1
Phoenix Clo. HU8 21 H4
Pickering Rd. HU4 30 B4
Pickering Vw. HU4 30 C4
Pier St. HU1 9 E6
Pilots Way. HU9 9 G5
Pine Mdws. HU10 16 D3
Pine Wk. HU10 24 C2
Pinewood Gro. HU5 18 B5
Pitsford Clo. HU7 14 D5
Pitt St. HU3 19 E6
Plane St. HU3 31 E1
Plantation Dri,
  Anlaby Pk. HU4 30 B1
Plantation Dri,
  Nth Ferriby. HU14 27 A6
Plimsoll Way. HU9 9 H4
Plowden Rd. HU3 30 D2
Plym Gro. HU8 22 D1
Polo Villas,
  Perth St West. HU5 19 E5
Poolbank La. HU4 25 F4
Poorhouse La. HU9 34 D1
*Poplar Av,
  Reynoldson St. HU5 19 G3
Poplar Clo. HU4 30 A2
Poplar Ct. HU7 21 E2
Poplar Gro,
  Lorraine St. HU8 20 D5
Popple St. HU9 9 H3
Porlock Dri. HU7 14 D4
Porobello St. HU9 22 A5
Port Av. HU6 13 G2
Porter St. HU1 8 A6
Portland Pl. HU2 8 A3
Portland St. HU2 8 A2
Portmadoc Clo. HU7 14 C1
Posterngate. HU1 8 D5
Potterhill La. HU7 21 G2
*Premier Gro,
  Exmouth St. HU5 19 G2
Preston Rd,
  Bilton. HU11 23 H1
Preston Rd, Hull. HU9 22 A6
Prestongate. HU13 29 E4

*Pretoria Av,
  Seymour St. HU3 31 E2
Pretoria St. HU3 31 E1
*Pretoria Villas,
  De Grey St. HU5 19 H3
Primrose Dri. HU5 18 B5
Prince St. HU1 8 D5
Princes Av, Hull. HU3 19 G5
Princes Av,
  Northfield. HU13 29 E4
*Princes Av,
  Greek St. HU3 31 E2
Princes Dock St. HU1 8 D5
Princes Rd. HU5 19 H3
Princes St. HU2 9 E2
Princes Wharf. HU9 9 H4
Princess Gdns. HU5 19 G3
*Princess Gro,
  Ena St. HU3 31 G1
Priory Av. HU14 27 C7
Priory Clo. HU14 26 D3
Priory Cres. HU16 12 C3
Priory Fm Dri. HU4 30 C4
Priory Gro. HU4 30 C3
Priory Rd. HU5 18 C3
Priory Way. HU4 29 G4
Prospect Pl. HU9 9 G3
Prospect St. HU2 8 B2
Providence Row. HU2 32 A2
Prunus Av. HU10 17 G2
Pryme Ct. HU10 17 G5
Pryme St, Anlaby. HU10 17 G5
Pryme St, Hull. HU2 8 B2
Pulcroft Rd. HU13 28 D3
Pulman St. HU3 19 E5
Purton Gro. HU7 20 D1
Putney Pl. HU8 21 G3
Pykestone Pl. HU7 14 D3
Quantock Clo. HU3 32 A5
Quarrington Gro. HU7 14 C3
Quay St. HU1 8 D4
Quebec Dri. HU6 11 F4
Queen St. HU1 9 E5
Queen Victoria Sq. HU1 8 D4
Queens Alley. HU1 9 E5
Queens Clo. HU7 12 A4
Queens Dock Av. HU1 8 D3
Queens Dri. HU16 12 A4
Queens Gdns. HU5 19 H3
Queens Rd. HU5 19 H3
Queens Way. HU3 12 A3
Queensbury Way. HU14 26 D3
Queensgate St. HU3 31 G2
Queensway. HU13 28 D3
Quillcroft. HU6 12 D3
Quilter Av. HU4 30 A2
Quilter Dri. HU11 23 F1
Quintins Clo. HU9 33 F2
*Raglan Av,
  Raglan St. HU5 19 G2
Raglan St. HU5 19 G2
Railway St. HU1 8 D6
Rainham Clo. HU8 15 G6
Rainhill Rd. HU5 19 F3
Ramsden Pl. HU16 11 G4
Ramsgate Clo. HU8 15 G6
Randsfield Av. HU15 24 B4
Rangely Clo. HU7 14 D2
Rannoch Clo. HU7 14 C2
Ransome Way. HU15 24 C3
Rauceby Clo. HU7 14 C3
Raven St. HU9 33 F2
Ravenspur Rd. HU11 23 G1
Rawcliff Gro. HU4 30 C3
Rawling Way. HU3 31 H1
Raywell Clo. HU10 17 G4
Raywell St. HU2 8 B2
*Raywood Villas,
  Wellsted St. HU3 31 G2
Red Lion Ct. HU10 17 F5
Redbourne St. HU3 31 G2
Redcar St. HU8 9 G1
Redcliff Dri. HU14 27 B8
Redcliff Rd. HU13 28 D6
Redfern Clo. HU3 31 H2
Redland Dri. HU10 16 D2
Redmire Clo. HU7 14 C3
Redruth Clo. HU7 21 F1
Reed St. HU2 8 C3
Reedham Garth. HU4 29 G3
Reeds La. HU9 21 H6
Reeds La. HU9 22 A5
Reform St. HU2 8 C1
Regent Clo, Hull. HU3 31 H1
Regent Clo,
  Willerby. HU10 17 F2
Regina Cres. HU5 19 F3
Regis St. HU9 22 C5
Reigate Clo. HU8 22 B4
Reldene Dri. HU5 18 A5
Renfrew St. HU5 19 F5
Rensburg St. HU9 33 F1
Renton Ct. HU10 17 G5
Repton Dri. HU7 21 F3

Reservoir Rd. HU6 20 C4
Retford Gro. HU9 35 E1
Reynolds Clo. HU14 25 G4
Reynoldson St. HU5 19 G3
Rhodes St. HU3 31 E2
Rhyl Clo. HU7 14 C1
*Ribble Av,
  Tyne St. HU3 31 F3
Ribble St. HU3 31 F3
Ribblesdale. HU7 20 C2
Ribycourt. HU6 12 D3
Riccall Clo. HU6 13 E5
Richmond Rd. HU13 29 E3
Richmond St. HU5 19 F3
Ridgestone Av. HU11 23 E1
Ridgeway Rd. HU5 18 A5
Ridsdale. HU7 14 C6
Rillington Av. HU16 11 H4
Rimswell Gro. HU9 22 B6
Ringrose La. HU10 17 F5
Ringrose St. HU3 31 E2
Ringstead Garth. HU7 14 D4
Ripley Av,
  Perth St West. HU5 19 F5
Ripley Clo. HU6 13 F4
Riplingham Rd,
  Skidby. HU16 10 A3
Riplingham Rd,
  West Ella. HU16 16 A2
Ripon Way. HU9 33 E2
Risby Garth. HU16 10 B1
Rise Wk. HU3 31 G2
Riseby Gro. HU6 13 E6
Rishworth Clo. HU7 14 C2
Riston St. HU3 31 G2
River Gro. HU4 30 D4
River Vw. HU13 29 F4
Riversdale Rd. HU6 13 H5
*Riverside,
  Dene St. HU3 33 F1
Riverside Ct. HU13 28 D6
Riverview Av. HU14 27 B8
Riverview Gdns. HU7 20 A1
Rix Rd. HU7 20 D4
Robinson Row. HU1 8 D5
Roborough Clo. HU7 15 E6
Robson Av. HU6 13 G2
Robson Way. HU8 21 F1
Rochester Av. HU7 29 G2
Rockford Av. HU8 21 E5
Rockford Gro. HU8 20 D5
Rockley Ct. HU10 17 G5
Rodney Clo. HU3 8 C1
Roebank Arc. HU7 14 C3
Roger Garth. HU10 17 F2
Rokeby Av. HU4 30 A2
Rokeby Clo. HU4 30 A2
Rokeby Pk. HU4 30 A2
Rokel Ct. HU6 13 G6
*Roland Av,
  Arthur St. HU3 31 F2
Romford Gro. HU9 35 E1
Romney Gdns. HU5 20 A6
Ronaldsway Clo. HU9 22 B5
Rookley Clo. HU8 22 D3
Roper St. HU3 8 C5
Ropery St. HU3 32 A5
Rosamond St. HU3 31 G3
*Rose Av,
  Airlie St. HU3 31 F2
*Rose Villas,
  Middleburg St. HU9 33 F1
Roseberry St. HU3 19 E6
*Rosebery Av,
  Newland Av. HU5 19 H2
*Rosebury Villas,
  Rosmead St. HU9 33 F2
Rosedale. HU8 9 G1
*Rosedale,
  Morril St. HU9 33 F1
Rosedale Av. HU9 33 G1
Rosedale Gro. HU5 18 C4
*Rosedale Villas,
  Rosmead St. HU9 33 F2
*Rosedene Villas,
  Raglan St. HU5 19 G2
*Rosemead Villas,
  Rosmead St. HU9 33 F2
Rosemount Clo. HU6 13 G2
Rosewood Clo. HU4 18 A6
Rosey Row. HU3 33 E3
*Roslyn Av,
  Blenheim St. HU5 19 G4
Roslyn Rd. HU3 30 D1
Rosmead St. HU9 33 F2
*Rothesay Av,
  Exmouth St. HU5 19 G2
Rothesay Clo. HU9 33 G1
Rotterdam Rd. HU7 20 D3
Rowan Garth. HU16 10 B1
*Rowland Av,
  Field St. HU9 9 H1
Rowley Gro. HU3 13 E6
Rowlston Gro. HU9 22 A6
Roxburgh St. HU5 19 F5

Royal Wk. HU16 12 C5
Royale Ct. HU9 22 A5
Royston Gro. HU8 33 E1
Rudstone Gro. HU9 22 B6
Rufforth Garth. HU7 15 F6
Rugby St. HU3 31 G3
Rugmere Clo. HU3 31 H1
Runcorn Garth HU4 29 H2
*Ruskin Av, Ruskin St. HU3 31 F1
Ruskin St. HU3 31 F1
Russell St. HU2 8 B1
Rustenburg St. HU9 33 F1
Ruswarp Gro. HU6 12 D5
Rutherglen Dri. HU9 22 A5
Rutland Rd. HU5 18 D5
*Rydal Clo, De Grey St. HU5 19 H3
Rydal Gro. HU16 11 F2
Rydale Ct. HU5 20 A5
Ryde Av. HU5 20 A4
Ryde St. HU5 20 A5
Ryedale Gro. HU9 33 H1
Ryehill Gro. HU9 22 A5
*Ryland Villas, Rustenburg St. HU9 33 F1
Sable Clo. HU4 30 B5
Saddleworth Clo. HU7 14 C3
Saffrondale. HU10 17 F4
Sainsbury Way. HU4 29 G4
St Abbs Clo. HU9 9 F5
*St Albans Mt, St Michaels Mnt. HU6 13 H6
St Andrews Mnt. HU10 16 D3
*St Andrews Villas, Princes Rd. HU5 19 H3
St Andrews Way. HU8 21 E5
St Annes Dri. HU16 12 C5
St Annes Wk. HU15 25 E3
*St Augustines Av, Princes Rd. HU5 19 H3
St Augustines Ct. HU5 19 H2
*St Barnabas Ct, Boulevard. HU3 31 G3
St Barnabas Dri. HU14 26 E2
St Catherines Ct. HU5 20 A6
St Clements Pl. HU2 32 B1
St Davids Clo. HU16 12 C4
*St Edmunds Ct, Priory Dri. HU5 18 C3
*St Georges Av, St Georges Rd. HU3 31 F2
*St Georges Gro, St Georges Rd. HU3 31 F1
St Georges Rd. HU3 31 F1
*St Georges Ter, Redbourne St. HU3 31 G2
*St Georges Villas, Field St. HU9 9 H1
St Georges Wk. HU9 22 C6
St Heddas Ct. HU5 18 C3
St Helens Dri. HU15 25 E3
St Hilda St. HU5 32 A1
St Ives Clo. HU7 15 E6
St James Clo, Nth Carr. HU7 15 F6
St James Clo, Northfield. HU13 29 F4
St James Rd. HU14 25 G4
St James Sq. HU3 32 A5
St James St. HU3 32 A5
St Johns Ct. HU6 20 A4
*St Johns Ct, Queens Rd. HU5 19 H3
St Johns Gro. HU9 34 A1
St Johns Wk. HU13 29 F3
St Joseph Dri. HU4 30 B2
St Judes Ct. HU5 18 C3
St Julians Wells. HU10 17 E3
St Lawrence Av. HU16 11 G4
St Leonards Rd. HU5 20 A6
St Lukes St. HU3 8 A5
St Margarets Av. HU16 11 F2
St Margarets Clo. HU16 11 F3
St Margarets Ct. HU8 22 C2
St Mark St. HU8 32 D2
St Marks Sq. HU3 32 A5
St Martins Av. HU4 30 D1
St Marys Av. HU5 18 C1
St Marys Clo. HU15 24 B1
St Matthew St. HU3 31 G2
St Michaels Clo, Skidby. HU16 10 C1
St Michaels Clo, Sutton Ings. HU8 22 B3
St Michaels Mnt, Sculcoates. HU6 13 H6
St Michaels Mnt, Swanland. HU14 26 E3
St Monicas Ct. HU5 19 H2
St Nicholas Av. HU4 30 B4
St Nicholas Gdns. HU4 30 C4
St Pancras Clo. HU3 31 G2
…auls St. HU2 32 B1
…eter St. HU9 9 G3
St Peters Av. HU10 17 F4
St Peters Vw. HU11 23 F2
St Silas St. HU2 32 C1
St Stephens Clo. HU10 16 D1
St Stephens Sq. HU1 8 A3
St Stephens St. HU1 8 A3
St Thomas More Rd. HU4 29 G1
St Thomass Grange. HU5 18 C3
*St Wilfreds Av, Greek St. HU3 31 E2
St Wilfreds Ter. HU5 19 G2
*Salisbury Av, Springburn St. HU3 31 E2
*Salisbury Gdns, Raglan St. HU5 19 G2
Salisbury St, Hessle. HU13 29 E4
Salisbury St, Newland Pk. HU5 19 G3
*Salisbury Villas, Holland St. HU9 33 F1
Salmon Gro. HU6 19 G1
Salt End La. HU12 35 G5
Saltash Rd. HU4 29 G3
*Saltburn Av, Folkestone St. HU5 20 A6
Saltburn St. HU3 31 E3
Saltford Av. HU9 35 F1
Saltgrounds Rd. HU15 24 A5
Salthouse La. HU1 9 F3
Salthouse Rd. HU8 21 G2
Salton Av. HU5 18 D2
Salvesen Way. HU3 31 E4
Samman Clo. HU10 17 E4
Sancton Clo. HU16 11 F2
Sandale Ct. HU5 18 D4
Sandfield Dri. HU15 24 C4
Sandford Clo. HU7 14 C5
*Sandlemere Clo, Edinburgh St. HU3 31 E2
Sandpiper Way. HU4 30 A5
Sandringham Clo. HU16 11 H2
*Sandringham Ct, Sandringham St. HU3 31 F1
Sandringham St. HU3 31 F1
*Sandringham Villas, Wells St. HU3 31 F2
Sands Ct. HU14 27 B7
Sands La. HU15 24 B1
Sandy Point. HU11 23 E3
Sandycroft Clo. HU5 18 A3
Saner St. HU3 31 G1
Saners Clo. HU16 12 A6
Sapperton Clo. HU7 14 C3
Sapphire Gro. HU3 31 F3
*Savannah Av, Minton St. HU5 20 A4
Savery St. HU9 21 G6
Savile Ct. HU1 8 C4
Savile St. HU1 8 C4
Savoy Rd. HU8 21 H4
Sawston Av. HU5 18 B3
Saxby Rd. HU8 22 B3
Saxcourt. HU6 12 D3
*Saxon Villas, Eastbourne St. HU3 31 F2
Saxondale. HU4 18 A6
Scalby Gro. HU5 18 C5
Scale La. HU1 9 E4
Scale La Staith. HU1 9 E4
Scampton Garth. HU7 15 F6
Scarborough St. HU3 31 F3
Scarrington Cres. HU4 18 A6
Scarrow Clo. HU3 19 F6
School La, Kirk Ella. HU10 16 D3
School La, Nth Ferriby. HU14 27 C7
School St. HU1 8 C3
Schooner Ct. HU4 29 H2
Scotney Clo. HU2 32 B1
Scott St. HU2 8 D1
Scott St Bri. HU2 9 E1
Scotts Sq. HU1 9 E6
Sculcoates La. HU5 20 A6
Seafield Av. HU9 22 A5
Seagran Av. HU13 29 F2
*Seamer Av, Mulgrave St. HU8 9 F1
Seaton Gro. HU4 30 D2
Seaton Rd. HU13 29 F3
Sedbergh Av. HU5 18 C1
Sedgebrook Gro. HU7 14 C3
Seel Ct. HU13 29 G4
Sefton St. HU3 31 G3
Segrave Gro. HU5 18 C5
Selby St. HU3 31 F2
*Selinas Cres, Rosmead St. HU9 33 F2
Selkirk St. HU5 19 F5
Selsy Clo. HU5 20 A5
Selworthy Clo. HU7 14 D4
Selwyn Av. HU14 27 C7
Setterwood Garth. HU10 17 F3
Setting Cres. HU5 18 C3
Setting Rd. HU5 18 C3
Severn St. HU8 33 E1
*Severn Villas, Rosmead St. HU9 33 F2
Sewer La. HU1 8 D6
Sextant Rd. HU6 13 H3
Seymour St. HU3 31 E2
Shaftesbury Av. HU8 22 A4
Shakespeare Clo. HU2 8 A1
Shannon Rd. HU8 22 C2
Shardeloes. HU11 23 E2
Sharpe St. HU5 19 G2
Shaw St. HU9 9 H2
Sheldon Clo. HU7 4 D5
Shelley Av. HU9 22 D6
Sherbrooke Av. HU5 18 D1
Sherburn St. HU9 33 F1
Sherwood Av. HU9 33 G1
*Sherwood Av, Welbeck St. HU5 19 G5
Sherwood Ct. HU11 23 E2
Sherwood Dri. HU4 18 A6
*Sherwood Gro, Perth St West. HU5 19 F5
Shetland Clo. HU8 21 G1
Shevington Wk. HU8 22 D2
Shipley Clo. HU9 22 C6
Shipton Clo. HU9 22 D3
*Shirley Av, Perth St West. HU5 19 F5
Shoreditch Clo. HU8 22 A3
Shorewell Clo. HU8 22 D2
Short St. HU1 8 A3
Shropshire Clo. HU5 18 C4
Sibelius Rd. HU4 30 A3
Sidings Ct. HU15 24 B5
Sidmouth St. HU5 19 G2
Silsden Av. HU6 13 H3
Silver St. HU1 9 E4
*Silverdale, Rosmead St. HU9 33 F2
Silverdale Rd. HU6 13 H5
Silvester St. HU1 8 D3
Sinclair Cres. HU8 21 H2
Sirius Clo. HU3 31 F2
Sittingbourne Clo. HU8 15 G6
Sitwell St. HU8 32 D2
Skelton Av. HU5 18 D2
Skerne Gro. HU9 22 B6
Skidby Gro. HU6 13 E6
Skilgate Clo. HU7 14 C4
Skillings La. HU15 24 B5
Skipwith Clo. HU6 13 G5
Skirbeck Rd. HU8 21 F3
Sleaford Av. HU9 23 E6
Sledmere Gro. HU4 30 D2
Sleights Clo. HU3 19 F6
Slingsby Clo. HU5 18 C2
Snainton Gro. HU5 18 C5
Snowdon Way. HU7 14 C1
Snowhill Clo. HU7 14 D2
Snuff Mill La. HU16 12 B5
Soffham Clo. HU7 14 C5
Somerden Rd. HU9 35 F3
Somerscales St. HU2 32 A2
*Somerset Av, Franklin St. HU9 33 E2
Somerset St. HU3 31 F2
Sorbbs Ct. HU3 32 A4
Sorbus Vw. HU5 18 B5
South Bridge Rd. HU9 9 F6
South Church Side. HU1 8 D5
South Clo. HU6 13 G4
South Ella Dri. HU10 17 E3
South Ella Way. HU10 16 D4
South La. HU13 29 E4
South St, Hull. HU1 8 B3
South St, Cottingham. HU16 11 H3
South Vw, Anlaby Pk. HU4 30 A1
South Vw, Willerby. HU10 17 E2
*South Vw, Sherburn St. HU9 33 F1
Southburn Av. HU5 18 D6
Southcoates Av. HU9 21 H6
Southcoats La. HU9 33 F1
Southcroft Clo. HU8 21 G1
Southern Dri. HU4 30 B2
Southfield Ct. HU16 11 G4
Southfield Dri. HU14 27 B8
Southfield Rd. HU5 19 E3
Southfield. HU13 28 D5
Southgate. HU13 29 E4
Southgate Clo. HU10 17 F1
Southgates La. HU9 33 G3
Southwell Av. HU9 35 F1
Southwood Av. HU16 11 G3
Southwood Dri. HU16 11 G3
Southwood Mws. HU16 11 G3
Southwood Rd. HU16 11 F3
Speeton Gro. HU5 18 C5
Spencer Clo. HU16 11 G3
Spencer Ct. HU3 31 G1
Spencer St. HU2 8 B2
Spencer Way. HU16 12 A4
Sperrin Clo. HU9 22 B4
Spinney Cft Clo. HU14 27 A6
Spinney Wk. HU4 30 B1
Spring Bank. HU2 8 A2
Spring Bank West. HU5 18 C5
Spring Gdns. HU8 21 G3
Spring Gdns E. HU4 30 A1
Spring Gdns Sth. HU4 30 A2
Spring Gdns W. HU4 30 A1
Spring Gro. HU3 19 F5
Spring St. HU2 8 A3
Spring Vale. HU11 23 E2
Springbok Clo. HU4 30 C5
Springburn St. HU3 31 E2
Springdale Clo. HU10 17 G3
Springfield Av. HU15 24 C3
Springfield Clo. HU15 25 E3
Springfield Rd. HU3 31 E1
*Springfield Villas, Pretoria St. HU3 31 E1
Springfield Way. HU10 17 F4
Springhead Av. HU5 17 H3
Springhead La. HU5 17 H4
Springville Av. HU13 29 F3
Spruce Rd. HU1 8 B6
Spyvee St. HU8 9 F2
Stafford St. HU2 32 B1
Staines Clo. HU8 22 B4
Staiths Rd. HU12 35 H3
Stalybridge Av. HU9 23 E6
Stamford Gro. HU9 35 E1
Stanbury Rd. HU6 13 H3
Standidge Dri. HU8 22 B3
Stanhope Av. HU9 21 H5
Stanley St. HU3 19 H6
Stannington Dri. HU8 22 D1
Stansfield Clo. HU9 35 E1
Stapleford Clo. HU9 23 E6
Starboard Av. HU6 13 H3
Starella Gro. HU3 31 F3
Startforth Wk. HU5 18 D1
Station Dri. HU5 32 A1
Station Rd, Brough. HU15 24 A4
Station Rd, Cottingham. HU16 12 B4
Station Rd, Hessle. HU13 29 E5
Station Rd, Nth Ferriby. HU14 27 B7
Station Wk. HU16 12 B5
Statton Vw. HU14 27 B7
Staveley Rd. HU9 22 C4
Staxton Ct. HU9 33 G2
Steeton Av. HU6 13 H3
Stembridge Clo. HU9 23 E6
Stephenson Ct. HU5 19 F3
Stephenson St. HU9 33 G1
Stephensons Wk. HU16 12 C5
Stepney La. HU5 20 A6
Stewart Garth. HU16 11 F2
Steynburg St. HU9 33 F1
Stiles Cft. HU14 26 F3
Stirling St. HU3 31 E1
*Stirling Villas, Stirling St. HU3 31 E1
Stockbridge Av. HU9 35 E1
Stockbridge Pk. HU15 24 B1
Stockbridge Rd. HU15 24 A1
Stockholm Rd. HU7 20 B2
Stockleigh Clo. HU7 14 C5
Stockwell Gro. HU9 35 E2
Stoke St. HU2 32 A2
Stonebridge Av. HU9 23 E6
Stoneferry Rd. HU8 20 D4
Stonegate Clo. HU8 21 G1
Stonepit Rd. HU15 25 F2
Stonesdale. HU7 20 C2
Stornaway Sq. HU8 21 H1
Story St. HU1 8 C3
Strand Clo. HU2 32 A2
Strathcona Av. HU5 18 D1
*Strathcona Villas, Ceylon St. HU9 34 C3
Strathearn St. HU5 19 H2
Strathmore Av. HU6 13 H5
Stratton Clo. HU8 22 C1
Stratton Pk. HU14 26 E3
Strawberry St. HU9 9 H2
Strensall Rd. HU5 18 B4
Strickland St. HU3 31 H3
Strines Gro. HU8 21 G1
Stromness Way. HU8 21 H1
Stroud Cres East. HU7 14 D6
Stroud Cres West. HU7 14 C6
Studley St. HU8 33 E2
Subway St. HU3 31 G3
Suffolk St. HU5 20 A5
Suffolk Ter, Suffolk St. HU5 20 A5
Sullivan Rd. HU4 30 A3
Summergangs Rd. HU8 21 F5
Summergroves Way. HU4 30 A5
Sunbeam Rd. HU4 30 C2
Sunningdale Rd, Hessle. HU13 29 E3
Sunningdale Rd, Dairycoates. HU4 30 D3
Sunny Bank. HU3 19 F5
*Sunny Dene, De la Pole Av. HU3 19 E5
*Sunny Gro, Sharpe St. HU5 19 G2
*Sunnydene Villas, Estcourt St. HU9 33 F2
Surbiton Clo. HU8 21 H3
Surrey Garth. HU4 29 H1
Sussex Clo. HU5 18 C4
Sutherland Av. HU6 13 G5
Sutton Clo. HU7 15 E6
Sutton Ct. HU8 21 G2
Sutton Gdns. HU7 20 D1
Sutton House Rd. HU8 21 G3
Sutton Rd, South Field. HU7 14 B1
Sutton Rd, Sutton-on-Hull. HU7 20 D2
Sutton St. HU3 19 H5
Sutton Way. HU9 22 C6
Swaddale Av. HU10 17 G1
Swainby Clo. HU8 21 F1
Swaledale Gro. HU9 33 G1
Swallowfields Way. HU4 30 A5
Swan St. HU2 32 C2
Swanella Gro. HU3 31 F3
Swanfield Rd. HU9 22 C5
Swanland Butts Clo. HU10 16 D5
Swanland Dale, West Ella. HU10 16 A2
Swanland Dale, Swanland. HU14 26 C1
Swanland Garth. HU14 27 C5
Swanland Gro. HU6 13 E6
Swanland Hill. HU14 27 C6
Swanland Rd. HU13 28 C3
Swanland Way. HU16 11 F3
Sweet Dews Gro. HU9 33 F2
Swinburne St. HU8 21 F6
Swinderby Garth. HU7 15 E5
Swinegate. HU13 29 E4
Swithin Clo. HU4 29 G3
Swyndham St. HU3 19 H6
Sycamore Clo. HU5 18 B5
Sycamore Ct. HU5 19 H4
*Sydney Gro, Tyne St. HU3 31 F3
Sykes Clo. HU10 17 G5
Sykes St. HU2 8 D2
Sylvia Clo. HU6 13 E5
Symersley Rd. HU5 18 A5
Symons Clo. HU2 32 B2
Syssons Way. HU5 20 B4
Tadman St. HU3 31 H3
Tall Trees. HU13 28 C2
Tamar Gro. HU8 22 D1
Tanfield Gro. HU9 22 C5
Tarran Av. HU6 13 G2
Taunton Rd. HU4 29 G2
Tavistock St. HU5 19 G2
Taylor Av. HU9 22 D5
Teddington Clo. HU8 21 G2
Tedworth Rd. HU9 22 D3
Tees Gro. HU8 22 C1
Teesdale. HU9 33 G1
Telford St. HU9 21 G6
*Temperance Av, Clyde St. HU3 31 E2
Temple Clo. HU15 25 F3
Temple St. HU5 32 A1
Temple Wk. HU15 25 F3
Temsdale. HU7 20 C2
Tennison Mws. HU16 11 H2
Tenterden Clo. HU7 20 D2
Tern Gro. HU8 22 D3
Terry St. HU3 32 A1
Thanet Rd. HU9 22 D2
Thaxted Clo. HU8 22 C2
The Avenue, Anlaby. HU10 17 G4
The Avenue, Cottingham. HU16 11 H2
The Avenue, Kirk Ella. HU10 16 D4
The Avenue, Sutton-on-Hull. HU7 21 G2
*The Avenue, Clyde St. HU3 31 E2
*The Avenue Crescent, Albemarle St. HU3 31 F
*The Beeches, Goddard Av. HU5 19 G
*The Beeches, Sidmouth St. HU5 19 G

The Broadway. HU9 22 A5
The Burrs. HU15 24 A4
*The Cedars, Sidmouth St. HU5 19 G2
The Chestnuts. HU5 19 G3
The Circle. HU13 29 E3
The Close, Cottingham. HU16 11 G4
The Close, Sutton Ings. HU7 21 G2
The Close, Willerby. HU10 17 G2
The Coachings. HU13 28 D6
The Covet. HU16 12 B5
The Crescent. HU15 25 E3
*The Crescent, Melrose St. HU3 31 E2
The Croft. HU7 14 B6
The Dales. HU11 11 E2
The Drey. HU14 26 D4
*The Elms, Melrose St. HU3 31 E2
The Fairway. HU8 16 B3
The Fairways. HU8 22 A2
The Gardens, Hull. HU3 31 G2
The Gardens, Sutton-on-Hull. HU7 21 F2
The Garth. HU16 11 H3
The Glen. HU10 16 C2
The Green, Brough. HU15 24 C3
The Green, Welton. HU15 25 E3
The Greenway, Anlaby Pk. HU4 30 B1
The Greenway, Gipsyville. HU4 30 D3
The Grove. HU8 21 E5
The Haven. HU9 9 G4
The Hawthorns. HU8 21 G1
The Hollies. HU10 17 F1
*The Hollies, Sidmouth St. HU5 19 G2
The Hourne. HU13 29 E3
*The Laurels, Raglan St. HU5 19 G2
The Lawns, Anlaby. HU10 · 17 F4
The Lawns, Sutton-on-Hull. HU7 21 F2
The Limes. HU5 19 G3
The Link. HU4 30 B2
The Lunds. HU16 16 D5
The Meadows, West Carr. HU7 14 A6
The Meadows, West Ella. HU16 16 B3
The Mews. HU3 31 H2
The Mount. HU13 28 D6
The Newlands. HU5 19 G1
The Octagon. HU10 17 G2
The Orchard. HU9 22 C4
The Oval, Anlaby. HU10 17 F3
The Oval, Elloughton. HU15 24 C3
The Oval, Garden Village. HU8 21 E6
The Paddock, Anlaby Pk. HU4 30 A2
The Paddock, Cottingham. HU16 12 B5
The Paddock, Nth Ferriby. HU14 27 B5
The Paddock, Swanland. HU14 26 E2
The Paddocks. HU10 16 C4
The Parade. HU5 19 H4
The Parkway, Cottingham. HU16 11 G4
The Parkway, Willerby. HU10 17 F3
The Pickerings. HU14 27 B8
The Poplars. HU5 19 G3
The Poplars, Durham St. HU8 21 E6
The Quadrant. HU6 13 E6
The Queensway. HU6 13 G3
The Quorum. HU4 30 D4
The Redwoods. HU10 16 D1
The Ridings, Anlaby. HU10 17 H3
The Ridings, Cottingham. HU16 11 F2
The Ridings, Nth Ferriby. HU14 27 C8
The Rise. HU14 27 B6
The Roundway. HU4 30 A2
The Rydales. HU5 20 A5
The Spinney, Cottingham. HU16 12 A5
The Spinney, Swanland. HU14 26 D2
The Square. HU13 29 E4
The Triangle. HU14 27 A7
The Vale. HU10 16 D4

The Weir. HU13 29 E4
The Willows. HU13 29 E2
The Wolds. HU16 11 F2
The Woodlands, Cottingham. HU16 11 G2
The Woodlands, Newland Pk. HU5 19 G3
Thearne Clo. HU5 19 H2
Thirlby Wk. HU5 18 C1
*Thirlmere Av, Wellsted St. HU3 31 G2
Thistleton Gdns. HU5 20 B6
Thomas St, Holderness Rd. HU9 33 F3
Thomas St, Crowle St. HU9 9 H2
Thoresby St. HU5 19 G5
Thorgill Gro. HU5 19 G5
Thornbridge Rd. HU9 22 B4
Thorndale. HU7 14 B6
Thornhams Way. HU15 24 C1
Thornhill Av. HU8 21 F4
*Thornton Av, Newstead St. HU5 19 F5
Thornton Clo. HU13 28 D4
*Thornton Dale, New Bridge Rd. HU9 33 H2
Thornton Ter. HU9 33 F1
Thornwick Av. HU10 17 F3
Thornwick Clo. HU3 31 H2
Thornwood Av. HU5 18 A6
Thorpe Rd. HU15 24 C4
Thorpepark Rd. HU6 13 E3
Thurlstone Av. HU7 14 C2
Thwaite St. HU16 12 B5
Tichbourne Clo. HU3 31 H2
Tickton Gro. HU6 19 E1
Tilbury Rd. HU4 29 G2
Tilworth Rd. HU8 22 A4
Tinley Clo. HU16 12 A4
Tison Garth. HU10 17 G5
Tithe Rd. HU12 35 G1
Tiverton Rd. HU7 14 C5
Todds Clo. HU14 26 F3
Togo Cres, Eastbourne St. HU3 31 F2
Tom Potts Row. HU14 26 A1
Tonbridge Gro. HU9 23 E6
Toogood St. HU2 32 C2
Topaz Gro. HU3 31 F3
Topcliffe Garth. HU7 15 F6
Torchill Clo. HU10 16 D5
Torpoint Dri. HU4 29 H2
*Torquay Villas, Rosmead St. HU9 33 F2
Torridge Gro. HU8 22 D2
Torrington St. HU5 19 H2
*Torrington Villas, Franklin St. HU9 33 F2
Tottenham Clo. HU8 21 H3
Towan Clo. HU7 14 C5
Tower Hill. HU13 29 E3
Tower Hill Dri. HU13 29 E4
Tower Hill Mws. HU13 29 E4
Tower House La. HU12 35 G3
Tower St. HU9 9 F5
Tower Vw. HU10 16 D6
Townsend Dri. HU16 11 G3
Trafalgar St. HU3 8 A1
Trafford Rd. HU10 17 F3
Train Av. HU6 13 G3
Tranby Av. HU16 28 C3
Tranby La, Kirk Ella. HU10 17 E5
Tranby La, Swanland. HU14 26 D3
Tranby Ride. HU10 16 D6
Tranmere Clo. HU3 31 G2
Travis Rd. HU16 11 H4
Trawden Clo. HU7 14 C2
Tremayne Av. HU15 24 A4
Trevor St. HU2 8 D1
Triangle Dri. HU14 27 A7
Trinity Clo. HU1 8 D5
Trinity Garth. HU16 10 B1
Trinity Gro, Hessle. HU13 29 E3
Trinity Gro, Newland Pk. HU5 19 G3
Trinity Gro, Hull. HU9 33 H1
Trinity House La. HU1 9 E4
Trinity House Yd. HU1 8 D4
Trinity St. HU3 19 H6
Trippet St. HU2 9 E2
Triton Rd. HU3 31 H3
Troutsdale Gro. HU9 34 A1
Trundle St. HU1 8 D5
Truro Clo. HU7 21 F1
Tudor Dri. HU4 30 D2
Tudor Dri. HU6 13 F3
Tunis St. HU5 20 A6
Turmar Vw. HU11 23 G1
Turners La. HU14 27 B6
Turners Clo. HU9 23 F6
Tweed Gro. HU8 22 C3

Tween Dykes Rd. HU7 21 F2
Twickenham Clo. HU8 22 B3
Twyford Clo. HU9 23 E6
Tyne St. HU3 31 F3
Tynedale. HU7 20 C2
Tynemouth St. HU2 8 C3
Ullswater Clo. HU8 21 F4
*Ulrome Ct, Granswick Gro. HU9 34 B1
Ulverston Rd. HU4 29 G2
Union St. HU2 8 C3
Upavon Garth. HU7 15 F6
Upper Union St. HU1 8 B5
Upton St. HU8 33 E1
Uxbridge Gro. HU9 23 E6
Valentine Clo. HU8 29 G3
Valiant Dri. HU4 22 D4
Valley Dri. HU10 16 C4
Vane St. HU2 8 A1
Vaughan Rd. HU13 29 E5
Vauxhall Gro. HU3 31 H2
Ventnor St. HU5 19 G2
*Vera Gro, Stirling St. HU3 31 E1
*Vermont Cres, Worthing St. HU5 20 A5
Vermont St. HU5 20 A5
*Vermont Villas, Vermont St. HU5 20 A5
Vernon St. HU1 8 D3
Vicar La. HU1 9 E5
*Vicarage Ct, Vicarage Gdns. HU15 24 E1
Vicarage Gdns. HU15 24 B1
Vicarage La. HU13 29 E4
Viceroy Clo. HU2 32 B2
Victor St. HU9 33 F2
*Victoria Av, Willerby. HU10 16 D1
Victoria Av, Newland Pk. HU5 19 F3
*Victoria Av, Alfonso St. HU3 31 G2
*Victoria Av, Granville St. HU3 31 F2
*Victoria Av, Rustenburg St. HU9 33 F1
*Victoria Av, Stepney La. HU5 20 A6
Victoria Av, Wellsted St. HU3 31 G2
Victoria Gdns. HU5 19 F3
Victoria Sq. HU5 19 G3
Victoria St. HU13 29 G4
*Victoria Villas, Clyde St. HU3 31 E2
Victorias Way. HU16 12 B4
Viking Clo. HU8 16 D1
Village Rd. HU8 21 F6
Vincent Clo. HU4 29 G3
Vine Clo. HU16 11 H1
*Virginia Cres, Worthing St. HU5 20 A5
Voases Clo. HU10 17 F5
Voases La. HU10 17 F5
Vulcan St. HU6 20 B4
Waddington Clo. HU5 19 G1
Wadebridge Gro. HU9 35 E1
Wadham St. HU8 33 H1
Wadhurst Clo. HU7 20 D2
Wadsworth Av. HU6 13 H3
Wainfleet Av. HU16 11 H3
Wake Av. HU16 11 G4
Wakefield Av. HU9 22 C6
Walcot St. HU3 31 G3
Waldegrave Av. HU8 22 A4
Walgrave St. HU5 19 G1
Walker St. HU3 8 A5
Waller St. HU9 33 E2
Walliker St. HU3 31 F1
Walmsley St. HU2 8 A1
Walnut Clo. HU6 12 C6
Walnut Tree Way. HU4 30 C4
Walrus Arc. HU13 29 E4
Walsall Garth. HU4 29 G1
Walters Ter. HU5 19 H2
Waltham St. HU1 8 C3
Walton St. HU3 19 F5
Walworth Clo. HU5 21 H2
Wanless St. HU8 12 B3
Wansbeck Rd. HU8 22 C1
Wansford Gro. HU9 34 B1
Ward Av. HU11 23 F1
Wareham Clo. HU7 21 E2
Warneford Gdns. HU5 19 F4
Warwick St. HU9 9 H3
Warwicks Clo. HU5 18 C4
Wascana Clo. HU4 29 H2
Wasdale Grn. HU16 12 A4
Washington St. HU5 20 A5
*Washington Villas, Rosmead St. HU9 33 F2
Wassand St. HU3 31 H3
Waterdale. HU7 14 B6

Waterhouse La. HU1 8 C5
Waterloo St. HU2 32 B1
Waterworks La. HU11 23 E2
Wath Gro. HU8 33 E1
Watson Av. HU9 - 22 D6
Watson St. HU7 21 F2
Watt St. HU9 21 G6
Watton Gro. HU6 13 G4
Wauldby Clo. HU10 17 F4
Wauldby Vw. HU14 26 E2
Waveney Rd. HU8 22 C2
Waverley St. HU1 8 A6
*Wawne Gro, Alexandra Rd. HU5 20 A5
Wawne Lodge. HU7 14 C2
Wawne Rd. HU7 14 C3
Weardale. HU7 14 B6
Weaver Gro. HU8 22 C1
Weelsby Way. HU13 28 C3
Weeton Clo. HU11 23 G1
Weighton Gro. HU6 13 E6
Welbeck St. HU5 19 G5
Welburn Wk. HU4 18 A6
Welbury Gro. HU9 23 E6
Well La. HU10 17 E1
Welland Rd. HU8 22 C1
Wellburn Gro. HU5 18 D3
Wellesley Av. HU6 20 A4
*Wellesley Villas, Middleburg St. HU9 33 F1
Wellington La. HU3 32 A2
Wellington St. HU1 8 D6
Wells St. HU3 31 F2
Wellsted St. HU3 31 G2
Welshpool Clo. HU7 14 C1
Welton Av. HU10 16 D6
Welton Gro. HU6 13 E6
Welton Low Rd. HU15 24 F2
Welton Old Rd. HU15 25 F3
Welton Rd. HU5 24 A4
Welwyn Park Av. HU6 13 H4
Welwyn Park Dri. HU6 13 H4
Welwyn Park Gro. HU6 13 H4
Wembley Park Av. HU8 22 A3
Wendron Clo. HU7 21 F1
Wenlock Ct. HU3 31 F1
Wenlock St. HU3 19 H6
*Wenlock Ter, Rustenburg St. HU9 33 F1
Wenning Gro. HU8 22 D1
Wensley Av. HU6 18 D1
Wensleydale. HU7 14 C6
Wentworth Clo. HU10 17 G3
Wentworth Way. HU9 33 F3
Wesley Ct. HU3 31 G2
West Carr La. HU7 20 C2
West Carr La. HU7 20 C3
West Dock Av. HU3 31 G3
West Dock St. HU3 31 F4
West Ella Rd. HU10 16 D4
West Ella Way. HU10 16 D4
West End. HU14 26 D3
West End Rd. HU16 11 G2
West Grn. HU16 11 G2
West Gro. HU4 30 C3
West Hill. HU13 29 E3
West Leys Pk. HU14 26 D4
West Leys Rd. HU14 26 C4
West Par. HU3 19 H5
West Par. HU3 31 H1
*West Park Gro, Granville St. HU3 31 F1
West Parklands Dri. HU7 27 B6
West St. HU1 8 B3
West Vw, Nth Ferriby. HU14 27 C7
West Vw, Sculcoates. HU5 20 A6
Westborough Way. HU4 18 A6
Westbourne Av, Hessle. HU13 29 E3
Westbourne Av, Stepney. HU5 19 F4
Westbourne Av, West. HU5 19 F4
Westbourne Gro. HU13 29 E3
Westbourne St. HU3 31 E2
Westcott St. HU8 21 F5
Westerdale Gro. HU9 33 H2
*Western Villas, Franklin St. HU9 33 E2
Western Villas, Rosmead St. HU9 33 F2
Westfield Clo. HU16 11 G3
Westfield La. HU14 26 C3
Westfield Pk. HU15 24 B3
Westfield Rise. HU13 28 D3
Westfield Rd, Anlaby Pk. HU4 30 C1
Westfield Rd, Cottingham. HU16 11 G3
Westfield Rd, Eppleworth. HU16 10 C4

Westgarth Av. HU6 13 E5
Westland Rd. HU10 16 C4
Westleigh Clo. HU7 14 C5
*Westmeath Av, Albemarle St. HU3 31 F2
Westminster Av. HU8 21 G5
Westmorland Av. HU2 32 C1
Westway Av. HU6 12 D4
Westwood Clo. HU7 21 F2
Westwood Dri. HU4 30 A1
Wetherby Clo. HU6 13 E4
Wexford Av. HU9 35 E1
Weymouth Clo. HU7 21 E2
Wharfdale Av. HU9 33 G1
Wharfedale, Goddard Av. HU5 19 G3
Wharncliffe Rd. HU5 19 F5
Wharram St. HU2 32 C1
Wheatcroft Av. HU10 17 G1
Wheatfield Clo. HU4 30 C5
Wheatley Gdns. HU8 21 F5
Wheeldale Clo. HU8 21 F1
Wheeler St. HU3 31 E1
Whernside Av. HU7 14 C3
Whitby Av. HU8 9 G1
*Whitby Gro, Rhodes St. HU3 31 E2
Whitby St. HU8 9 G1
White House Clo. HU10 16 D1
White St. HU3 31 E2
White Wk. HU10 16 D5
Whitefriargate. HU1 8 D4
Whitehall Gdns. HU5 19 F3
Whitehaven Av. HU5 19 G2
Whitehope Clo. HU7 14 D3
Whitethorn Way. HU8 21 F4
Whitstable Clo. HU8 15 G6
Whitstone Clo. HU7 14 C6
*Whittington Villas, Rosmead St. HU9 33 F2
Whitworth St. HU9 21 H6
Wickenby Garth. HU7 15 E6
Wikson St. HU9 9 G2
Wilbar Gro. HU5 19 F3
Wilberforce Dri. HU1 9 E3
Wilberforce St. HU3 32 A4
*Wilberforce Villas, Rosmead St. HU9 33 F2
Wilburn Clo. HU16 11 H2
Wilflete St. HU9 22 C5
Willerby Carr Clo. HU5 18 A4
Willerby Low Rd. HU10 10 D6
Willerby Rd. HU5 18 A5
Willesden Clo. HU8 21 H3
William St. HU1 8 A6
Williamson Way. HU10 16 C2
Willow Ct. HU10 17 F2
Willow Dri. HU10 17 F3
Willow Gro. HU5 19 H3
Willowdale. HU7 14 B6
Willowfield. HU6 13 F5
Willows Av. HU9 22 A5
Wilson St. HU10 17 F5

Wilton St. HU8 9 H1
Wiltshire Rd. HU4 31 E3
Wimbledon Clo. HU8 22 A3
Wimborne Clo. HU7 21 E1
Winchester Av. HU9 22 C4
Winchester Clo. HU9 22 C4
Wincolmlee. HU2 9 E1
Windle Av. HU6 13 G3
Windsor Av. HU10 17 F4
*Windsor Av, Exmouth St. HU5 19 G2
Windsor Clo. HU16 12 A5
Windsor Rd. HU5 19 F4
Winestead Gro. HU8 22 B6
Wingfield Rd. HU9 22 C5
Winscar Croft. HU8 21 G1
Winston Dri. HU16 11 H3
Winthorpe Rd. HU13 29 F2
Wistow Gro. HU10 30 C2
Witham. HU9 9 F2
Withernsea St. HU8 32 D1
Witty St. HU3 31 H4
Wivern Rd. HU9 22 D5
Woburn St. HU3 31 E3
Wold Rd. HU5 18 A3
Wold Vw. HU15 24 C3
Woldcarr Rd. HU3 30 D1
Wolfe Clo. HU16 11 G4
Wolfreton Dri. HU10 17 G5
Wolfreton Garth. HU10 17 E3
Wolfreton La. HU10 17 G2
Wolfreton Rd. HU10 17 F4
Wolfreton Villas. HU10 17 G4
Wood Dri. HU14 27 A7

Wood La. HU16 12 A6
Wood Vw. HU14 26 E2
Woodbine Clo. HU2 32 B2
*Woodbine Villas,
 Reynoldson St. HU5 19 G3
Woodcock St. HU3 31 E3
Woodcroft Av. HU6 13 E6
Woodfield La. HU13 28 C4
Woodgate La. HU5 19 E5
Woodgate Rd. HU5 19 E5
Woodgates Clo. HU14 27 B6
Woodgates La. HU14 27 B6
Woodgates Mnt. HU14 27 B5
Woodhall St. HU8 20 D6
Woodhill Clo. HU10 17 F4
Woodhill Rise. HU13 28 C4
Woodland Av. HU15 24 C3
Woodland Dri. HU10 16 D5
Woodland End. HU4 30 B2
*Woodland Villas,
 Rensburg St. HU9 33 F1
Woodlands Rise. HU14 27 B6
Woodlands Road. HU5 18 B5
Woodleigh Dri. HU7 21 F3
Woods La. HU1 8 B6
Woodside. HU13 28 D3
Woodstock Clo. HU14 11 G3
Woolsthorpe Gro. HU7 14 C3
Woolwich Dri. HU4 29 H3
Worcester Rd. HU5 18 B4
Worcestershire Clo. HU5 18 C4
Wordsworth St. HU8 21 F6
Workington Av. HU4 30 A1
Worsboro Clo. HU8 21 G1
Worship St. HU2 8 D2
Worthing St. HU5 20 A4
Wright St. HU2 8 B2
Wrygarth Av. HU15 24 B4
*Wyke Av,
 Springbank St. HU3 31 E2
Wyke St. HU9 33 F3
Wykeham Clo. HU8 21 F1
Wynburg St. HU9 33 F1
Wyton Rd. HU9 22 A6
Yarmouth Av. HU4 29 G3
Yatesbury Garth. HU7 14 D5
Yeadon Garth. HU7 15 E6
Yewtree Dri. HU5 18 A6
Yiewsley Clo. HU8 21 G2
York La. HU10 13 E3
York Rd. HU6 10 D6
York St. HU2 32 C2
*York Ter,
 Rustenburg St. HU9 33 F1
York Way. HU10 16 D1
Yorkshire Clo. HU5 18 C4
Zeigfeld Ct. HU3 22 B5
Zetland St. HU3 31 F2

BARTON-UPON-HUMBER

Antelope Rd. DN18 39 F2
Appleyard Dri. DN18 39 B4
Ardent Ct. DN18 39 F2
Bardney Ct. DN18 39 E4
Barrow Rd. DN18 39 D3
Baysgarth Vw. DN18 39 E4
Beacon Av. DN18 39 C3
Beck Hill. DN18 39 D3
Beretun Grn. DN18 39 C3
Birchdale. DN18 39 C4
Blyth Ct. DN18 39 E4
Bowmandale. DN18 39 C3
Bradwell Clo. DN18 39 B3
Brigg Rd. DN18 39 D3
Burgate. DN18 38 D2
Butts Rd. DN18 39 C2
Caister Clo. DN18 39 D3
Castle Ct. DN18 39 D3
Castledyke Sth. DN18 39 D3
Castledyke West. DN18 39 C4
Catherine St. DN18 38 D2
Chapel La. DN18 39 C2
Church Vw. DN18 39 D3
Cladsons La. DN18 39 C1
Cliff Gro. DN18 39 C3
Cornhill Dri. DN18 39 E3
Cott La. DN18 38 D2
Council Ter. DN18 39 C2
Dam Rd. DN18 39 B1
Danson Clo. DN18 39 E3
Duncan Dri. DN18 39 C2
East Acridge. DN18 39 D2
East Gro. DN18 39 E2
Eastfield Rd. DN18 39 D4
Elmdale. DN18 39 C4
Fairfield Clo. DN18 39 E1
Falkland Way. DN18 39 E1
Far Ings Rd. DN18 39 A1
Ferriby Rd. DN18 39 B2
?kle La. DN18 39 C2

Fleetgate. DN18 39 C2
Forkedale. DN18 39 B3
George St. DN18 39 D3
Georgina St. DN18 39 B4
Glebe Way. DN18 39 F2
Globe Clo. DN18 39 E3
Goddard Clo. DN18 39 B4
Goodhand Clo. DN18 39 E4
Grange Av. DN18 39 C3
Greenway. DN18 39 E2
*Halls Ct,
 Kingston Vw. DN18 39 E4
Harrier Rd. DN18 39 E1
Harrowdyke. DN18 39 C3
Haven Rd. DN18 39 B2
Hawthorn Gate. DN18 39 D4
Hewsons La. DN18 39 C1
High St. DN18 39 C2
Highfield Cres. DN18 39 E3
Hillside Dri. DN18 39 B3
*Holgate Ct,
 Kingston Vw. DN18 39 E4
Holydyke. DN18 39 C2
Hopper Clo. DN18 39 E4
Horkstow Rd. DN18 39 C4
Humber Bri App. DN18 39 A3
Humber Rd. DN18 39 C1
Humber Rd. DN18 39 B3
Humber Vw. DN18 39 B2
Hungate. DN18 39 C2
INDUSTRIAL ESTATES:
 Humber Bridge
 Ind Est. DN18 39 E1
Junction Sq. DN18 39 C2
King St. DN18 39 D3
Kings Garth. DN18 39 E3
Kingston Vw. DN18 39 E4
Lincoln Rd. DN18 39 C2
Lodge Av. DN18 39 C3
Lunns Cres. DN18 39 C2
Maltby La. DN18 39 C1
Maltkiln Rd. DN18 39 D3
Market La. DN18 39 D2
Marsh La. DN18 39 C4
Marsh St. DN18 38 D2
Masons Ct. DN18 39 B4
Meadow Dri. DN18 39 E3
Millbrook Way. DN18 39 E4
Millfields. DN18 39 C4
Milson Clo. DN18 39 B3
Mount Av. DN18 39 C3
Newport St. DN18 39 C2
Nicholas La. DN18 39 B4
Nicholson Dri. DN18 39 E3
Norman Av. DN18 39 E3
Nursery Clo. DN18 39 E2
Orchard Clo. DN18 39 D4
Overton St. DN18 39 C2
Park Av. DN18 39 C3
Park Vw. DN18 39 D4
Parkdale. DN18 39 C4
Pasture Rd Nth. DN18 39 D1
Pasture Rd Sth. DN18 39 D2
Pasture Rd. DN18 39 D2
Pelham Clo. DN18 39 B3
Pitman Av. DN18 39 B4
Ponds Way. DN18 39 B2
Preston La. DN18 39 D3
Priestgate. DN18 39 D3
*Prince Charles Dri,
 Qn Elizabeth Wy. DN18 39 D4
Prince Phillip Dri. DN18 39 E4
Princess Dri. DN18 39 E4
Providence Cres. DN18 39 C3
Queen Elizabeth
 Way. DN18 39 E4
Queen St. DN18 38 D2
Queens Av. DN18 38 D2
Ramsden Av. DN18 39 C3
Ravendale. DN18 39 E4
Regency Ct. DN18 39 B2
River Vw. DN18 39 C1
Ropery La. DN18 39 C1
St Marys La. DN18 39 D3
St Peters Clo. DN18 39 C2
Saxon Clo. DN18 39 E3
Sedge Clo. DN18 39 D2
Shadwell Rd. DN18 39 B2
Soutergate. DN18 38 D2
Stable La. DN18 39 B1
Stephen Cres. DN18 39 C4
Stevenson Way. DN18 39 C4
Summerdale. DN18 39 C4
Sunnybank. DN18 39 B3
Tangarth Clo. DN18 39 D2
The Bridges. DN18 39 B4
Tofts Rd. DN18 39 B4
Treece Gdns. DN18 39 B2
*Uppleby Clo,
 Kingston Vw. DN18 39 E4
Varah Clo. DN18 39 B4
Vestry La. DN18 39 D3
Victoria Dri. DN18 39 C2
Victory Rd. DN18 39 E1
Warrendale. DN18 39 B3
Warwick Dri. DN18 39 B4

Waterside Rd. DN18 39 C1
Webb Clo. DN18 39 B4
Welton Clo. DN18 39 C4
West Acridge. DN18 39 D2
West Gro. DN18 39 B2
Western Dri. DN18 39 B2
Westfield Rd. DN18 39 B2
Whiston Way. DN18 39 E2
Whitecross St. DN18 39 D3
Willow Dri. DN18 39 E2
Yarborough Ct. DN18 39 E4

BEVERLEY

Admiral Walker Rd. HU17 4 D5
Albert Ter. HU17 4 D4
Albion Ct. HU17 5 G4
Alpha Av. HU17 4 C1
Annie Reed Rd. HU17 5 G4
Arden Rd. HU17 5 F3
Ash Clo. HU17 5 E1
Ashmole Wk. HU17 5 F2
Athelstan Rd. HU17 5 E3
Bainton Clo. HU17 4 C3
Balmoral Dri. HU17 4 D6
Barmston Clo. HU17 5 G3
Barmston Rd. HU17 5 G3
Barnes Clo. HU17 5 F4
Bartlett Av. HU17 4 D4
Beaver Rd. HU17 5 F4
Beck Vw Rd. HU17 5 G4
Beckside. HU17 5 F5
Beckside Nth. HU17 5 F4
Beech Av. HU17 5 E1
Belprin Rd. HU17 5 F3
Berkeley Dri. HU17 4 D6
Beverley By-Pass. HU17 4 B1
Beverley Parklands. HU17 5 G1
Bielby Dri. HU17 5 F4
Birch Clo. HU17 5 E1
Bishops Croft. HU17 4 D4
Bleach Yard La. HU17 4 C2
Blenheim Rd. HU17 4 D6
Blucher La. HU17 5 E4
Bramble Garth. HU17 5 E1
Brereton Clo. HU17 4 D2
Brimley. HU17 4 B2
Brooklands Clo. HU17 5 E2
Burden Clo. HU17 5 F2
Burden Rd. HU17 5 E2
Burnaby Clo. HU17 4 D2
Burney Clo. HU17 4 B2
Burton Rd. HU17 4 B2
Butcher Row. HU17 4 D4
Butt La. HU17 4 D6
Butterfly Mdws. HU17 4 D1
Carlton St. HU17 4 D4
Carr Clo. HU17 5 F4
Cartwright La. HU17 4 C5
Cavendish Dri. HU17 4 D6
Central Av. HU17 4 C5
Champney Rd. HU17 4 D4
Chantry La. HU17 5 E4
Chatsworth Clo. HU17 4 D6
Cherry Garth. HU17 5 E4
Cherry Tree La. HU17 5 E3
Cherry Tree Ter. HU17 5 F4
Chestnut Av. HU17 5 E1
Chestnut Clo. HU17 5 E2
Church Grn. HU17 4 A2
Church Rd. HU17 4 A2
Church Vw. HU17 5 F4
Clare Ct. HU17 5 G4
Coltman Av. HU17 5 E2
Conington Av. HU17 5 G4
Constitution Hill. HU17 4 A1
Coombs Yd. HU17 4 D3
Cooper St. HU17 4 D2
Copandale Rd. HU17 4 D4
Corn Hill. HU17 4 D4
Coronation Clo. HU17 5 F3
Corporation Rd. HU17 4 D3
Cottage Mws. HU17 5 E3
Crab Tree Wk. HU17 5 F4
Cranshaw Av. HU17 4 D2
Crathorne Rd. HU17 4 D4
Cross St. HU17 5 F3
Crosskill Clo. HU17 5 F2
Crowther Clo. HU17 4 D1
Curlew Clo. HU17 4 C1
Danesway. HU17 5 F3
Dennet Rd. HU17 5 F4
Denton St. HU17 5 E5
Dill Dri. HU17 4 D4
Dog & Duck La. HU17 5 E4
Dominican Wk. HU17 4 B1
Driffield Rd. HU17 4 D6
Durham Mews. HU17 4 C1
Dyet La. HU17 4 C1
East Clo. HU17 4 C3
East La. HU17 5 F2
Eastfield Clo. HU17 5 E4
Eastgate. HU17

Eden Clo. HU17 4 C2
Eden Rd. HU17 4 C2
Ellerker Rd. HU17 4 C5
Elm Clo. HU17 4 C2
Elmsall Dri. HU17 4 B2
Empson Ter. HU17 4 D4
Figham Link Rd. HU17 5 F5
Figham Rd. HU17 5 F5
Figham Springs
 Way. HU17 5 E6
Finch Pk. HU17 4 C2
Fisher Sq. HU17 4 D4
Flemingate. HU17 5 E5
Fotherby Wk. HU17 5 F2
Friars La. HU17 5 E4
*Friary Wk.
 Eastgate. HU17 5 E4
Gallows La. HU17 4 C3
George St. HU17 5 F4
Godbold Clo. HU17 5 F4
Goodfell Rd. HU17 5 F1
Goths La. HU17 5 E3
Grayburn La. HU17 4 D4
Greenwood Av. HU17 5 E3
Greenwood Gdns. HU17 5 E1
Greyfriars Cres. HU17 4 C5
Grosvenor Pl. HU17 4 C5
Grove Clo. HU17 4 D2
Grove Pk. HU17 4 D2
Grovehill Rd. HU17 5 G4
Grovehill. HU17 5 H4
Guildford Clo. HU17 4 D6
Hall Garth Way. HU17 5 E5
Hammond Rd. HU17 5 F4
Hanover Ct. HU17 4 D4
Harewood. HU17 4 B2
Hargreave Clo. HU17 4 D2
Hawthorne Garth. HU17 5 E1
Hengate. HU17 4 D4
Highfield Rd. HU17 5 E2
Highgate. HU17 4 B1
Hill Crest. HU17 4 B1
Hillcrest Dri. HU17 4 C1
Hobson Ct. HU17 5 E4
Hodgson Av. HU17 5 E4
Holderness Cres. HU17 5 E4
Holme Church La. HU17 5 F3
Hotham Sq. HU17 5 E4
Hull Bridge Rd. HU17 5 E2
Hull Rd. HU17 5 F5
Hull Rd. HU17 4 C3
Hurn Vw. HU17 4 C3
INDUSTRIAL ESTATES:
 Acorn Ind Est. HU17 5 H3
 Grovhill Ind Est. HU17 5 G4
 Swinemoor
 Ind Est. HU17 5 G3
Jefferson Clo. HU17 5 G5
Keel Clo. HU17 4 D5
Keldgate. HU17 4 B6
Keldgate Rd. HU17 5 F1
Kilvin Dri. HU17 4 D3
Kings Sq. HU17 5 G4
Kirkholme Way. HU17 4 D5
Kitchen La. HU17 5 E3
Knights Way. HU17 5 E1
Laburnam Dri. HU17 4 D4
Ladygate. HU17 4 D4
Lairgate. HU17 4 D4
Landress La. HU17 5 E3
Langdale Av. HU17 4 C3
Langholm Clo. HU17 5 E2
Laughton Rd. HU17 4 D6
Leathley Clo. HU17 5 E1
Lilac Av. HU17 5 E1
Lime Tree Av. HU17 5 E1
Lincoln Way. HU17 4 D6
Linton Clo. HU17 4 D6
Long La. HU17 5 E5
Longcroft Pk. HU17 4 B2
Lord Roberts Rd. HU17 4 D4
Lowfield Rd. HU17 5 E1
Lyndhurst Clo. HU17 5 F4
Mace Vw. HU17 4 D5
Mallard Clo. HU17 4 D1
Malton Rd. HU17 4 A1
Manor Clo. HU17 4 D3
Manor Pk. HU17 4 D3
Manor Rd. HU17 4 D3
Maple Dri. HU17 5 E2
Marsh Dri. HU17 5 E6
Martin St. HU17 5 F4
Meadow Bank. HU17 5 E1
Melrose Pk. HU17 4 D5
Middle La. HU17 5 E3
Middleton Clo. HU17 5 F3
Mill La. HU17 5 E3
Mill La Clo. HU17 5 E4
Mill View Rd. HU17 5 F5
Minster Av. HU17 5 E5
Minster Ct. HU17 4 D5
Minster Moorgate. HU17 4 D5
Minster Vw. HU17 4 D6
Minster Yd Nth. HU17 5 E5
Minster Yd Sth. HU17 5 E5

Mint Wk. HU17 5 E6
Mintfield Rd. HU17 5 F4
Molescroft. HU17 4 C1
Molescroft Av. HU17 4 C1
Molescroft Dri. HU17 4 C1
Molescroft Mews. HU17 4 B1
Molescroft Pk. HU17 4 C2
Molescroft Rd. HU17 4 B1
Morton La. HU17 4 D4
Napier Clo. HU17 4 D3
Neville Av. HU17 5 F3
New Walk. HU17 4 C3
New Walkergate. HU17 4 D4
Newbald Rd. HU17 4 A5
Newbegin. HU17 4 D4
Newton Dri. HU17 4 D4
Nicholson Clo. HU17 5 G3
Nolloth Cres. HU17 5 E3
Norfolk St. HU17 4 C3
North Bar Within. HU17 4 D4
North Bar Without. HU17 4 C4
Northfield Rd. HU17 4 B2
Norton St. HU17 4 D4
Norwich Ct. HU17 4 C4
Norwood. HU17 4 D3
Norwood Dale. HU17 4 D3
Norwood Far Gro. HU17 5 E2
Norwood Gro. HU17 4 D2
Nursery Gdns. HU17 5 E4
Oak Clo. HU17 5 F1
Oak Tree Clo. HU17 4 C2
Oak Tree Gro. HU17 4 C2
Old Beck Rd. HU17 4 C2
Old Manor Lawns. HU17 5 H4
Orchard Garth. HU17 4 C2
Outer Trinities. HU17 5 E4
Park Av. HU17 4 D3
Parkfield. HU17 4 C3
Pasture La. HU17 4 C4
Pasture Ter. HU17 5 F2
Pennyman Rd. HU17 4 C1
Pighill La. HU17 5 E3
Pinfolds. HU17 5 E3
Plantation Clo. HU17 5 G4
Poplar Dri. HU17 5 E2
Princes Gdns. HU17 4 D4
Priory Rd. HU17 5 E4
Quaker La. HU17 4 C4
Queens Rd. HU17 5 F3
Queensgate. HU17 4 D5
Railway St. HU17 5 E4
Regent St. HU17 4 D4
Riding Fields Sq. HU17 5 E3
Risby Pl. HU17 4 D6
Rokeby Clo. HU17 4 D2
Rosemary Way. HU17 5 F5
Routh Av. HU17 5 F3
Rowan Av. HU17 5 E1
Royal Garth. HU17 4 C6
Sage Clo. HU17 5 E5
St Andrew St. HU17 5 E5
St Annes Clo. HU17 5 E5
*St Davids Clo,
 Hallgarth Way. HU17 5 E5
St Ellens Ct. HU17 5 E4
St Giles Croft. HU17 4 D4
St John St. HU17 5 E5
St Leonards Rd. HU17 4 B1
St Martins Ct. HU17 4 D5
St Marys Clo. HU17 4 C1
St Marys Ter. HU17 4 C4
St Marys Wk. HU17 4 C3
St Matthews Dri. HU17 4 D1
St Nicholas Dri. HU17 5 F1
St Nicholas Rd. HU17 5 F1
Samman Rd. HU17 5 F1
Sample Av. HU17 5 E4
Saturday Mkt. HU17 4 D4
Savile Clo. HU17 4 D2
Saxon Rise. HU17 4 C4
Schofield Av. HU17 5 F3
School La. HU17 4 C4
Scrubwood La. HU17 4 C6
Seven Corners La. HU17 4 C4
Sheldrake Way. HU17 5 E1
Shorthill Cft. HU17 4 C4
Sigston Rd. HU17 5 F3
Sloe La. HU17 4 C4
Smedley Clo. HU17 5 F5
Southfield Dri. HU17 4 C3
Sow Hill. HU17 4 D4
Spark Mill La. HU17 5 F4
Springdale Way. HU17 4 D1
Springfield Dri. HU17 5 E1
Storkhill Rd. HU17 5 F4
Swinemoor La. HU17 5 G4
Symmons Clo. HU17 5 E3
Tandyke Way. HU17 4 D1
Tardrew Clo. HU17 5 F5
The Causeway. HU17 5
The Cedar Grn. HU17 5
The Copse. HU17 5
The Croft. HU17 5
The Dell. HU17 5
The Glade. HU17 5